Pig Tails 'n Breadfruit

Pig Tails 'n Breadfruit

A CULINARY MEMOIR BY

Austin Clarke

THE NEW PRESS NEW YORK

Originally published in Canada by Random House of Canada, Ltd., 1999

Published in the United States by The New Press, New York, 2000

Distributed by W. W. Norton & Company, Inc., New York

ISBN 1-56584-580-3 (hc.)

CIP data available

The New Press was established in 1990 as a not-for-profit alternative to the large, commercial publishing houses currently dominating the book publishing industry. The New Press operates in the public interest rather than for private gain, and is committed to publishing, in innovative ways, works of educational, cultural, and community value that are often deemed insufficiently profitable.

The New Press, 450 West 41st Street, 6th floor, New York, NY 10036

www.thenewpress.com

Printed in the United States of America

9 8 7 6 5 4 3 2 1

To Clifton Arthur Luke,

my brother,

who knows more about cooking . . .

Table of Contents

Introduction

food. It is a word that defines my life. Not food in the sense of "hot-cuisine," as my mother called that kind of French sophistication with sauces and garlic, in her characteristic dismissive prejudice against food cooked by Europeans, especially the French. "What do French-people know about cooking food?"

It was her final judgement, and the last nail in the coffin of any pretentiousness I would have about food; about learning French cooking; and about learning the French language in high school, at Combermere School for Boys in Barbados, where I grew up.

"We talking about *food*, boy. Food!"

Food: that thing that went into my stomach in such delightfully huge quantities, and that had such delectable taste and smell, when I was a boy. Taste and smell are important distinctions in my mother's definition of what food really is. Food to her, as to me, is something very special, almost supernatural. Something that blends in with the culture of the place I was born. In Barbados, we like to eat food — just like to eat it. And whatever it is that we cook, we call it food, in the sense that any combination of any ingredients ("ingreasements"), of whatever quality, that we put into a pot and cook is food — giving this food no more sophistication or pretence about its distinctiveness to make us use fancy words and fancy attitudes and call this kind of food, and the time the food is eaten, by names to give it more appeal, myth and class than it deserves. And the things we use to cook this food with — the ingreasements or the seasonings — are not specified, or singled out, for special mention. This kind of food is simple, basic food. For instance, a T-bone steak or a rib roast are both called "a piece o' beef." Any part of the pig is a "piece o' pork." Food, then, is food. Pure and simple and good.

Nor are we restricted by precise measurements. Cooking food is not characterized by strict attention to ounces and grams, cups and litres. A pinch of this and a pinch of that added to a pot, at first by trial and error, and then perfected through history and constant usage, from one generation to the next, is the way I remember food being cooked. The fingers and hands are the implements for measurement.

Taste is the thing. And touch. Tasting and touching.

So, we are talking about cooking food with feeling. Feeling is stretched to include "feeling-up" the food: touching the fish; pulling out the entrails of a chicken with your fingers; peeling potatoes and slicing them with a knife while holding them in your hand — not using a gadget that ensures precision of cut and duplication of each slice.

And when we come to flour and the making of bread, then the hands do all the work. There is no heavy-duty electric mixer, just the heel of the palm of the hand, which is enough to knead the flour into dough.

It is ironical to be suggesting a book about food cooked in Barbados, because in every self-respecting Barbadian household the woman (who does most of the cooking, whether she is wife, daughter or maid) would not be caught dead with a cookbook. To read a cookbook would suggest that she has not retained what her mother taught her; that she does not know how to cook; that she does not know how to take care of her man; that her mother had neglected to teach her how to "handle herself" in the kitchen, how "to do things" properly.

There was never, and still is not, a cookbook in my mother's house.

In this idea of having to be shown how to cook from the pages of a book lies an ineradicable assault upon the culture and character of Barbadian women. Instead, both culture and the ability of a woman to handle herself in the kitchen are based upon the handing down through time of methods of cooking. Things handed down must be remembered, word for word, so as not to dilute "the way of cooking"; and in this way they are expected to retain their essential essence of perfection and legitimacy.

One family would cook food in one fixed and traditional way; another family would cook the very same food in a slightly less traditional manner. But the results would, basically, be the same. For instance, in the making of sweetbread, or coconut bread, one family might mix the flour in with the ground coconut. Another family might concentrate the coconut in a vein in the dough, so that the coconut stretches throughout the length of the loaf itself. This way, with each slice, the person eating the sweetbread is gratified by a generous portion of coconut (mixed with brown sugar, nutmeg and other spices), giving the slice a more tantalizingly satisfying flavour.

Middle-class women make sweetbread that tends to be lightweight. Lower-class women make sweetbread that is heavier and "sweeter," and we call their bread "heavy-sweets," not referring to the sugar used in its preparation, but meaning that it tastes better. Barbadians use the term "sweet" to express our love and appreciation for all food that is cooked appetizingly.

"My mother does-cook sweet-sweet-sweet," I used to tell my friends. The older boys, with more learned references and wider experiences, talked about a different kind of "sweetness," which had nothing to do with food. Their appreciation of "sweetness" referred to girls whose attention they hoped to attract. And they would claim, "Boy, I know she sweet! She *look* sweet!"

The men in the neighbourhood, models our mothers warned us against but models nevertheless, ruled over us with their tales of even bigger sweetnesses. These men sometimes imparted to us in strictest secrecy their own knowledge of sweetness in women. They voiced profound and frightening conclusions. "Man, she is the most sweetest woman that I have ever make a thing with, or *known* in my born days." We accepted their conclusions, and we kept their confidence as our own knowledge. We understood, even with our puny experience, precisely what "known" meant. Barbados, at that time, was a very Christian-minded island. All of us read the Bible, and not only on Sundays. And as boys we underlined all those verses that contained the words "known" and "begat."

By now you might have realized that I do not use terms like the "cooking of dishes" or "recipes." The word "recipe" did not exist in the Barbados of my youth. As a boy I was surrounded by women — mother, countless aunts, women-cousins and all the neighbourhood women, my mother's friends — women who were all continuously involved in some confounding and miraculous feat in the kitchen. In all that time, and with all those women, I never once heard one of them use the word "recipe."

I am quite small at the time of my earliest memories of cooking food. I am about eight years old, and in Second Form at the Combermere School for Boys. My mother never had any great respect for my smallness or youth as a determiner of the amount or bigness of the tasks she gave me to do. So, from the time I could hold a fork, I had to help her mash English potatoes. With the other kind of fork, the agricultural fork, she made me help her prepare her kitchen garden for planting cucumber, "punkin," pigeon peas, tomatoes, lettuce, sweet potatoes and yams.

This distribution of labour, not only in the cooking of food but including all household chores, is what brought me closer to cooking. It prepared me for my great fondness for food — cooking it and eating it — learning everything about it at the apron-strings, so to speak, of my mother and other women.

At this time I lived in a village named St. Matthias. We called it Sin-Matthias. It was bounded on one side by the Marine Hotel, where "tourisses," mainly from England, danced in an open-air ballroom on Old Year's Night and threw their balloons over the high walls to us at the last stroke of midnight.

Sin-Matthias was bounded on another side by the Marine Pasture, an area of grass where we played cricket and football; and on another side still by the adjoining village, whose name was Harewood's Village, after the first Barbadian family of Harewoods, who settled on this parcel of land. This was on a hill, famous for delicious duncks, a local fruit that we stole from the stubby trees and ate in secret.

On its most important and significant side, the village was bounded by the Sin-Matthias Anglican Church, in whose choir, later on, from the age of nine, I sang soprano. On the seaside end of the church was my elementary school, Sin-Matthias School for Boys; on the inland side, the Sin-Matthias School for Girls.

My village was also next door to the Hastings Rocks, on whose esplanade black nursemaids walked huge blue perambulators filled with white English children, pushing them face-first into the intoxicating breeze from the sea to quell their screams. These prams held the offspring of the local Barbadian whites, as well as those of the few foreigners, as we called them, who came to the island to rule over us, in school, in church, in the civil service, in the police force and in banks.

I am talking about Barbados in the late 1930s and early 1940s. It was a place of severe order and discipline and training, to make you know your place: respect for elders, and for the schoolmaster, and for policemen — to say nothing of aunts and uncles and neighbours, and my mother's innumerable friends, all of whom could (and did) chastise me on the spot for the slightest disobedience.

The most frequent act of disobedience, or bad manners, as I was told, was not to recognize a woman or a man who had visited our house the night before, and not to say

"Good morning, sir" or "Good morning, ma'am" before they recognized me, before my eyes and theirs "made four."

Sin-Matthias Village was about two miles from Town, which is what we called Bridgetown, our capital. And it was near the sea, about half a mile away. The most spectacular feature of our village was Reid's Dairy, from which we got fresh milk every morning. We went to the dairy, with an enamel cup or one made by the local tinsmith, for our milk. If we had lived farther from the dairy, the milk would have been delivered by horse-drawn cart.

There was always buttermilk, and cheese made by Mrs. Reid; and big black flies that came at you with such determination that you feared they would knock you down into cow-peed yard. And always the smell of urine and of cows and pigs. And on Saturday afternoons, the smell of fried liver and black pudding boiled in pots as large as those I had read about in books about witches and mysteries from the East. And boiled pigs' feet, and ears and snout for the making of souse, to be eaten with the black pudding.

Always, in this village, I was surrounded by women — not the girls with whom I played girls' games, like hide and hoop, or dollies, or house, but grown women. Severe and beautiful and strong; mysterious as the books I was reading; charitable, but willing on the slightest impulse to reprimand me for the smallest disregard of their status.

"I will tell your mother!" they said to me.

And I prepared my body and mind for the flogging I knew I would get when I reached home. It always seemed that the woman, whether neighbour or friend, would reach my mother first. Any plea of mine for mercy went unheeded. Nothing I could do.

"I will tell your mother, boy!"

In my household in Sin-Matthias Village, we lived in a kind of African compound, although none of us knew that term or understood that our arrangement of life had that African reference.

My mother was married to a man who lived with his mother — Gran, or Grans, we called her. My mother, understanding place and respect, also addressed her as Gran.

Gran ruled the roost. Her own daughter, Verona, a fierce, thin and trim unmarried woman with three children, called her Gran too. As I grew older, I would hear that Verona had her children from three different men and had refused to marry any one of them, those "worthless men!" She lived her life in full feminist independence, even before anybody in Barbados knew anything about single parents or independently spirited women.

Then there was Miss Edey, Gran's sister, another spinster, who wore starched white dresses and starched petticoats and a pleated starched apron every day of her life, as if she was morally reluctant to leave her profession of maid and housekeeper and wanted me, especially, to understand the importance of duty. She made toast every afternoon in her small room, on a small one-burner stove fed with kerosene, blackening her parlour with thick smoke and burning the toast, which always had to be scraped before she put thick layers of butter from Australia and jam from England on them. Every afternoon, at four. I told the time by the scraping of her toast.

And then we would have tea. She taught me to like books.

These women — Aunt Ronie and Miss Edey — were my allies. They intervened each time my mother's anger got the better of her, and would physically put their frail bodies between the whip (my mother's hand, a shoe, a tamarind rod) and me, shielding me as the whip rose and fell.

"Good Jesus Christ, Gladys! You intend to kill the boy?"

These women were always cooking, and my job was to provide the wood or chop down a branch of a tree to make kindling. Sometimes we used coal. As these women cooked, they talked about the food they were cooking and whether they should try a different assortment of spices, a different combination of ingreasements.

"A lil more hot pepper, this time, eh? What you think, boy? You think she could do with a pinch more? Last night the piece o' pork had-taste too fresh! Hand me the peppers, Tom!"

Tom is the name I am known by in Barbados.

Many times, I looked into the large, ugly, black iron pot — a *cauldron* in my small mind obsessed by mysteries and Grimm's fairy tales — and waited patiently for the succulent pieces of pig tail to cook. Sometimes, in a fit of compassion, a piece not quite cooked would be taken out and dropped into my hand. I would toss it from palm to palm in glee, and in pain from the searing heat.

"Take that, boy, to hold you till she done!"

And I would revel in the number of these surrounding women, knowing that many evenings I would eat four different dinners: food cooked by my mother, by Aunt Ronie, by Grans and by Miss Edey.

I liked food. Especially Miss Edey's sweetbread.

"This boy-child o' yours," she told my mother, "*loves* flour! It will make him strong, though!"

My mother's family lived a half-mile away. I would walk up the hill named after the Harewoods, round the Bath Corner — known as the University of the Bath Corner in later years, where men gathered every night of the week to discuss cricket and politics and "learning," arguing who was "the most brightest boy to ever live in this Bath Corner neighbourhood" — past the Christian Mission Church in God, turn left on Deighton Road and into Deighton Village.

The Kellys were a larger family, wealthier, light-skinned and living in a larger house. Cecilia, whom we called Dear Aunt, was the head of this family. Pricilla, her sister, whom we called Aunt Cilla, and uncles who lived in the country — in Sin-James, where I was born — were the other members of this family. Uncle Charles, Uncle Delbert and Uncle Tazz were fishermen. Tazz and Aunt Cilla were black like me and my mother. The others were either white or almost white — although at this time, when I was eight, these racial differences were not noticed by me, not mentioned, not important. I did not see my family in this harsh light of colour. Among the Kellys, Aunt Cilla played the same role of matriarch as Grans. She was married to a man who worked as a seaman in the engine room of a merchant ship.

The Kelly part of my family moved me from whatever status I had in Sin-Matthias Village to one of greater wealth, into a rambling, larger house, with a corddear tree high as the heavens in the yard. The house was filled with huge mahogany furniture: Demerara chairs on which I could lie to my full length and be buried in their cool comfort; large buffets like tombs; and European clothes closets, in the bottom drawers of which were toys that were brought from all over the world, with which I played whenever I visited Dear Aunt. There were the latest models of American and English and German cars, with rubber wheels that I sped across the boundless dark floors imitating four-laned highways and *autobahns* and *autopistas*. There were Dusenbergs, Chryslers, Rolls-Royces; and once I saw a Mercedes-Daimler, or a Benz-Daimler.

And always the women. Cooking, and telling stories that at night made my skin crawl with fear — stories of thieves and robbers, and "sinner-men" with five heads, and men with three legs who rode on donkeys made of steel. When darkness fell, I shuddered in the black shadows of stories about ghosts born in Barbados. Those women did not depend upon Grimm's fairy tales or Han Christian Andersen to bring my heart into my mouth.

In the late afternoon and evening, the hours after four o'clock, when it was cool and the breeze off the sea near to Sin-Matthias reached us in this short road, we would gather under the corddear tree and play games — me and my cousins, the children of my aunts. Hide and Hoop, London's Bridge is Falling Down, Hobbina-Bobbina Baby's Sneeze, and my favourite, Ship Sail, Sail Fast — a game we played by hiding kernels of roasted corn in our fists and challenging the other players to guess the correct number we held. If they guessed ten instead of the one I had in my hand, I would get ten of their roasted kernels to devour, with a smirk on my face.

This was a time of playing all day — even in school, where I was bright. A time of games. And in between playing games, during the day and in the early evening, it was a time to be summoned by the high-pitched voice of an aunt: "Food!"

In Dear Aunt's house were many framed pictures. I can still remember two of them, hung above the huge worm-eaten piano that was almost as large as Gran's house in Sin-Matthias; two oval mahogany frames, containing Dear Aunt herself and my uncle, a black man with the same complexion as myself, in a high collar that reached under his chin. Dear Aunt is dressed in white, with a ruff up to her ears, and I can see gold like drops of water sparkling from each ear, and round her collar, a chain. My uncle is stiff in black, and fierce; but there is also a smile on his face.

This smile I knew well. It shone whenever he came ashore from crossing the high seas, as he called his travels to England, to Africa, to Europe . . . when he would place the latest European model car into my hand.

"Come, Tom. Look at this Daimler. I got it in London. You ever see London?"

Only in books, although nobody said it was London. That would come later, when I took private tuition after normal school hours at Sin-Matthias Elementary School for Boys, when I heard about 1066, 1213, 1413, when I had to memorize the dates of battles fought on pages that came alive with bloodied Englishmen in helmets, wearing lances and spears. Hastings, Bannockburn, the Wars of the Roses. The only roses planted in the garden of the Kellys' house were red, so I took the side of the Englishmen who wore the red rose. No one in my village, whether Sin-Matthias or Deighton Road, had ever seen a white rose.

I remember the smell of the perfumes my young aunts wore, and the smell of the coconut oil they used to grease their legs. And I remember the smell of the loose-leaf English teas that were always boiling in a saucepan, and the smell of English marmalades, and the soft, delicate crunching of tea biscuits. But over all these things brought in the large leather grip across the high seas by my uncle, I preferred Miss Edey's burnt four o'clock toast.

My aunts in the Kelly household talked about food as they cooked, and teased me about the heat of a pot, sometimes daring me to put my hand in and "steal" a piece of the salt meat used for seasoning the rice. And from their casual discussion of the places our food came from, I learned a fascinating kind of geography and sociology. Rancid butter came from Australia. Thin, hard, bony, smelly cod fish, from Newfoundland. Biscuits and marmalades and toffees from England. And soaps for the skin. Apples wrapped in fine paper, from Canada. And "French letters," which the big boys talked about in secret, and called also "French leathers," came from France — although the box was marked "Manufactured in England."

I did not like Newfoundland, because of the poor quality of the salt fish they sent down to us. And I did not know, or feel, that Newfoundland could be in the same continent as Canada. Canada was better than Newfoundland. Canada sent us McIntoshes, which we called "English apples." Our own apples, "sugar apples" and "mammy apples," were good, and we ate them, of course, but the English apples were superior because they came from "Away."

So there were no recipes and no cookbooks. You might well ask, how then did these women provide the splendour of meals that could be smelled and remembered and yearned for from long distances away from their kitchens?

Before I answer this question, it might be better to begin by talking a little about kitchens in Barbados when

I was growing up — kitchens whose social status determined their construction, and perhaps what was cooked in them and by whom.

The kitchens of the very poor, at the time I was growing up in the mid-thirties, were three large stones placed on the ground or on an elevated base made of hard rock or concrete. These stones were placed roughly in the shape of a triangle and close enough together to accommodate the bottom of the cooking utensil.

The cooking utensil could be anything from a tin can, which we called a tinning or a tot, to a three-legged pot made out of iron, called a buck pot. The tinning was cleaned out after its initial use and taken to the tinsmith in the village, who would solder a lid, or two handles, onto the can. A kerosene tin (which may or may not have been used to hold kerosene oil; we just called it a kerosene tin) was square and not round. Canadians would call this kind of utensil a skillet.

The genius demanded in cooking on three stones is the management and regulation of the wood fire. In some cases the fuel was trash from dried sugar cane, or dried joints of sugar cane themselves. In order to regulate the heat for cooking, the pieces of cane would be taken from under the utensil or temporarily extinguished. In the hands of women not skilled, there was an easy chance that the food could be burned. Romances and marriages have ended, suddenly and tragically, when women could not rearrange the pieces of dried sugar cane under their pots with sufficient dexterity to prevent the food from being burnt. But the burning of food was not always regarded as a smear upon a woman's character and ability. In fact, burned food, which we called bun-bun, took on a cultural significance. The term "bun-bun" comes from "burnt," without the letter "r" and the letter "t", which at the end of a word is usually not pronounced. It is then hyphenated to give it significance, becoming "bu'n-bu'n." Hence, bun-bun. It is a term used in all strata of Barbadian society.

The bun-bun is the layer of food stuck to the bottom of the pot. It contains, in coagulated form, all the ingreasements that went into the "seas'ning" of the food: the oil, the pieces of meat that fell to the bottom, all the good things. And the present-day popularity of bun-bun suggests its culinary delectability, or sweetness. It is kept back and served to honoured guests or close friends.

The kitchen "stove" of the poor at that time was nothing more than stones arranged and placed in the backyard. It was outdoor cooking, something like a barbecue — but the term "barbecue" was never used in Barbados in those days. A barbecue is something slight, light-hearted, suggesting a party; but cooking, for these women, was drudgery, a serious function of daily family life.

With those not so poor, there were obviously variations that embellished these rudimentary arrangements for cooking food. Their kitchen stoves would be built about three or four feet off the ground, with a mixture of stone and cement; and in place of the three rock-stones, there would be a grate built from strong, thick wire, or thin strips of iron, with the stones cemented onto the flat top of the foundation. This kind of kitchen stove was large enough to accommodate at a time, two or three cooking utensils on it.

There is no comparing food cooked in these conditions with the "rough" kind cooked around camp-fires or in barbecues. This food was serious, as we say. It had to come out sweet, had to be a full meal, complete and with many parts. And it was cooked with fresh ingreasements, every day of the week; there were no fridges in those days.

Rain and sun and occasional hurricanes could not deter a woman from this essential work. The dexterity of the woman was also demonstrated by her being able to bake bread in this kind of kitchen. All that was needed to transform the stove into an oven was a cover for the particular cooking utensil she was using.

There is an explanation required at this point. I have been talking about kitchens and I ought to have been talking about stoves. But at the time I am talking about, we called it just that: the kitchen. What you cooked on was the most important thing in your kitchen.

Very often, in the area made for cooking, nothing apart from the three stones, or the grate, existed. The cooking utensils themselves, and the cups and plates and bowls, were kept in another part of the house. And the cooking contraption was normally outside the house, in the yard, where the danger of conflagration was reduced in proportion to its distance from the structure of the house itself, which was made of wood.

The kitchen (and now we have a better term, "the cooking area") of the middle class was normally inside the house. Even with the more general use of electricity, wood was used for cooking. In time, there were stoves that used gas, which came in a cylinder, supplied by the government.

The kitchen of the Plantation was a large structure attached to the main house, with a stove built from thick stone, a chimney pointing skyward from the top of the kitchen, and as many individual grates or elements as the household could afford. These kitchens would use for fuel the same things used by the other classes, but with the difference that they could afford "better" and a more regular supply of firewood for cooking than the lower classes. Wallaba wood was preferable; it gave a more constant heat.

This is not to say that food was not regularly burned in Plantation kitchens, or that bun-bun was not created. The Plantation owners and their families relished and understood the cultural aspects of bun-bun. After all, their cooks were the same women who used the three big rocks in their own backyards. And only the largeness of the cooking area and the quality of the ingreasements were superior in the Plantation houses. The skill of cooking remained constant, and it could become dexterous and gain celebrity because the facilities were better. But it was a well-known fact in Barbados that Plantation people, most of whom were white, did not put "enough seas'ning, nor salt and pepper in their food!" My mother used to say, "Their food too damn bland. Enough to give a person the belly! As if they're suffering from *low* blood pressure!"

These kitchens were dark places. Some were infested with stinging ants. Kitchens were places where hard work was performed; where thick smoke issued; where you got down on your hands and knees and spent hours cleaning the pots and pans, after soaking them for days. There was no hot-water tap to ease the washing of dishes, just cold water and blue soap and elbow grease. Blue soap was efficient, not only in cleaning utensils, but for the washing out of small boys' mouths that were blemished by fabrication and foul language.

"Boy, bring the blue soap here, and lemme wash out your damn mouth!"

This threat was made when I had imitated the language "picked up" from the bigger boys sitting on the Marine Pasture, where we played cricket, during a lull in the game, when the sun was hottest and the tall tales about girls would come out. I did not always know the real meaning of this language; but the beauty of its dialect, and the passion and violence the bigger boys put into their speech, peppering it with choice words, caused me to fall in love with more than its sound.

"You getting to have a dirty mouth!" Dear Aunt warned me. "Those bastards you're playing with are not your equals!" she added.

And I would be called inside, to sit in the dark house,

quiet and gloomy, smelling of camphor balls and old, rich mahogany. I would imagine I was imprisoned in one of those caves I read about in my private tuition classes; and I would read a book, and then burrow deeper into the bottom drawer of my personal treasure chest, filled with corsets and crinolines and antique cars from Europe. Finally, I would "take a rest" from the afternoon's unrelenting humidity.

I knew then, as I read the names of toy cars and the places of their manufacture, that I too would leave the hot island, and travel like my uncle on a merchant ship.

It was after the Second World War ended that money started coming into the villages in the returning pockets of men who had left to fight "the Nazzies"; who had left to cut sugar cane in Cuba and parts of the American South; who had left to work in the oilfields of Curaçao and Aruba; and who had found themselves on ships, sometimes illegally, and had jumped those ships when they anchored in American ports. There were women too, who had gone to Amurca as domestic servants and to Panama to cook for work crews. All this money that came into the villages contributed to making the houses bigger, conversation about Away more romantic and padded with lies, and the kitchens larger and more modern.

But some families did not become better off from this sudden importation and remittance of Yankee dollar bills and Dutch guilders. These families continued to cook their food on the same three blackened stones in the backyard.

For the most part, the middle classes — "those with get-up-and-get," as my mother labelled industriousness and ambition — found themselves suddenly using American technology, cooking on oil-burning stoves in kitchens that were no longer so desolate as those I was reading about in Victorian novels, in the Third Form at Combermere School for Boys.

My mother, Gladys Irene, and her husband, Fitz Herbert Luke, my stepfather, with whom I had lived since the age of one and a half years, now moved with the changing times. I was no longer a child of two families: one black, one white and half-white. We moved to the new, developing Village of Clapham, on a hill, looking back down upon the scorched grass of the Marine Pasture, at the blue sea whose waves had lapped my early beginning in Sin-Matthias and Deighton villages.

I was far from the sea and the beach — "that damn beach," where I was prevented from going to bathe with other boys because only "no-good boys spenn their time at the beach! You *not* becoming no fisherman, like your uncles Delbert and Tazz. I want you to be *somebody*!"

I don't know why my mother said this, because she loved all her brothers, full-brothers and half-brothers, those strong, big, handsome men with complexions reddened in the sun and from the salt in the sea water. And I do not know what caused her suddenly to despise the lives of those hard-working men, who could have passed for white if they wanted to. She was probably warning me about the reputation that men and boys who "lived on the beach" were beginning to have; those who, in anticipation of the years to come, and of the influx of "tourisses" from Canada and Montreal (we insisted upon the difference, just as we stuck to our bias about Canada and Newfoundland), were just beginning to be romanticized as "beach boys."

We now had our own house, wooden, unpainted, with a kitchen about one-quarter of the total size of the house itself; and with "land," not only around the house, but land, "the ground," a few acres, about half a mile away from the house, on which we planted sugar cane, eddoes, yams, sweet potatoes, mango trees, avocado trees and a million pigeon-pea trees. And corn, for my favourite game of Ship Sail, Sail Fast.

In the middle of the ground was a majestic mango tree, which did not bear fruit, but whose branches had grown in an arrangement suitable and comfortable as a small room, a "study" — a word I picked up at Combermere School for Boys — in which I would study later on, while attending Harrison College, the intractable texts of Latin and Roman history and English (at Advanced Level), and the Gospels of Sin-Matthew and Sin-John, and the commentaries that accompanied them. Here too, in this mango tree, I studied the physical and political geography of Canada, memorizing the names of the passes in the Rocky Mountains: Yellowknife, Kicking Horse and Crowsnest, knowledge I had garnered even before I had memorized the names of the eleven parishes of the island of Barbados.

I would look down from my study in the mango tree at the various colours of green, the canes, the cassava leaves, the leaves of the eight-weeks sweet potatoes, and I would transform them into waves and tides and currents of the sea surrounding the island, and sail upon the waves of the Atlantic Ocean that was the mother of the Caribbean Sea, and feel I was travelling on merchant ships, like my uncle.

Food and cooking in Barbados in the 1930s and 1940s had a ritualistic order of cultural significance. It originated in the days of economizing and slavery — two powerful factors in any consideration of Barbadian culture and folklore. Food rituals were based on the cultural intricacies of the availability of foodstuffs. The dynamics of social status and the strong effect it had on our lives, the communal nature of our villages, and the routine and schedule of harvesting the land and of the neighbourhood butcher determined when ingreasements and ground provisions were available to everyone, and therefore what you would eat on a given day of the week.

Because Barbados was a labouring society, most of its inhabitants, including women, worked in the fields. In my time, Saturday was the day to celebrate no work at all, or work for only half a day. Through this custom we began to count Saturday as the start of the week, and to associate Saturday with Sunday only in its specific relation to work and to food.

Saturday was the day for cleaning the house from top to bottom — sometimes to the extent of putting a new colour of paint on the wooden furniture; cleaning out the larder of all dust, cobwebs and black spots left by cockroaches and mice; using the cobweb-broom, high as a "stiltsman," to come face to face with dead scorpions and cockroaches and living spiders as large as man-eating beasts; washing every single piece of chinaware; polishing silvers, as my mother called all cutlery; and scrubbing all the floors in the house.

"On your hands and knees, boy! Get down on your two knees!" my mother said. "I want to see these floor shining. I want to see my face in them!"

We scrubbed these dealboard floors with blue soap and "white-head bush," a weed that grew wild and luscious, especially after a heavy rain. Our white-head bush ripped out stains three times better than Ajax, Javex and Dutch Cleanser rolled into one.

The food cooked on Saturdays was meant to reward the hard labour spent on the dealboard floors. And the food always centred around pork.

Pigs were killed on Saturdays by the neighbourhood "butcher." He was a man who had apparently decided one morning, on a whim, to start killing animals; and through trial and error, and by his persistence in this adventure, came to gain respectability with knife and sharpening stone. He began to call himself "butcher," and the neighbours grew accustomed to his boast and called him "butcher" too. He was usually a man of some means. He owned a few goats and sheep, perhaps a cow and pigs, which he reared and practised his butcheries on. Although he had no training in the anatomy of animals, he continued in this killing and hacking up and became skilled at it, and turned it into an occupation and a profession. Mr. Butcherman, my mother called him behind his back.

Barbadian colloquial terms like "to slice properly" or "to slice clean" or "to cut nice" are antonyms of another Barbadian term, "to butcher." The term "to butcher-up" was most likely born of the experience of some housewives who received their requested "cuts" of meat from the neighbourhood butcher in indistinguishable hunks. They might have received, from his practised hands, the spareribs attached to a piece of the rump, or a piece of the rump roast attached to a leg.

You would think that, growing up in an island — Barbadians say "in" an island, and not "on," as Canadians do — fish would be the premier staple of meat, but in Barbados it has always been pork. Now, with concerns about nutrition, and the fear of cholesterol and dropping dead from a heart attack, there is a greater consumption of chicken and fish. But in my day, and certainly in the house of my mother (who now lives in New Jersey), pork was the predominant meat. All self-respecting Barbadian homes served some cut of the pig on Saturdays, such as fried "harslick," or liver, from the freshly killed pig, with cou-

cou or "Bajan stew."

Harslick and cou-cou is a cultural dish in Barbados, something like "soul food" to African Americans. The harslick is floured, fried to an easy toughness, and served with lots of onions and tomatoes in its sauce.

The primary cultural food on Saturday is black pudding and souse. Black pudding is made from the entrails of the freshly killed pig, which are stuffed with seasoned, grated sweet potato and boiled slowly over a low heat. Souse is made from parts of the pig such as the trotters, the ears, the snout and some fat portions of the loin, which are seasoned, left to "draw" and served cold.

In St. Kitts and the Bahamas, two countries that pretend to be experts in this dish, souse is served hot or warm. Barbadians regard this custom as barbaric. We pride ourselves on being the inventors of pudding and souse, and we have taken it to its culinary elixir. We regard serving souse warm as evidence of the enormous cultural chasm that separates St. Kitts and the Bahamas from Barbados.

On each Saturday night, in every Barbadian home, was the ritual of "picking rice." You used your index finger and the thumb of the same hand, like an electric counter, to pick out the "weebulls," or weevils, specks and husks, dead, dried worms, and diminutive skeletons of insects peculiar to the jungles and wilds and paddy-fields of Demerara or Trinidad, from where the rice was imported.

"That ungodly place!" my mother called Demerara.

They practised witchcraft in Demerara, and they had poisonous snakes. Demerara was known as British Guiana before it gained its independence from the Mother Country and became Guyana.

Picking rice was not only a household function to ensure cleanliness, it was also a social event. A boy old enough, or lucky enough, to be courting was invited to the girl's home on Saturday night. While courting, he would pick rice, sometimes voluntarily, sometimes on the not-so-subtle hint of his prospective mother-in-law. Nevertheless, he would be ordered to leave the girl's house punctually at nine o'clock.

The suitor spent all his courting time in the company of the young lady *and* her mother, who acted as chaperone; and the passage of time, like the passing of hundreds of rice grains and weebulls through his fingers, made the courtship dramatically short. The monotony of extracting weebulls and blackened grains of rice was lessened by the chance that toes and feet and knees might touch under the table that bore the mountains of rice. And he would hope, no doubt, that the mountain of grains shining in the light made by the strong kerosene or gas lamp, or perhaps by the naked electric bulb hanging from the rafters (which denoted social and economic status), would take its slow time to be picked, and that the protective prospective mother-in-law would doze off and his fiancée would exploit her mother's temporary lapse in watchfulness and rub her knees against her suitor's, with stronger daring, and steal a kiss; and he would hope that his visit might be drawn out like the Sunday sermon of the English vicar of Sin-Matthias Anglican Church, at matins the following day. But the boy would have to be content with his slice of cake and pudding, baked and served by his looking-glass wife. Saturday was a day for baking sweetbread and pone. Pone is made from cassava that is grated and dried and made into a flour, with raisins, prunes, grated coconut and sugar, and is baked on a flat pan.

The best, or sweetest, food was eaten on Sunday. In olden times, and in a labouring-class society like Barbados, the woman of the house had time off on Saturday to collect all the ingreasements necessary for preparing her Sunday food. Even today, in changed and better circumstances, Sunday is still associated with the best food of the week.

My mother, who says her age is between eighty-one and ninety-one, and who has always insisted that her age is "none of your damn business!", makes it her business to impress me with the sharpness of her memory. Using memory and greater age as weapons of authority, she reminds me of the meals she cooked on Sundays sixty years ago.

Religiously, we had either baked pork, baked chicken or baked duck. "Baked chicken," she reminds me, "is one or two culinary levels below roast pork."

We kept ducks, along with fowls, sheep, a goat and pigs. And we kept turkeys. So there was nothing really festive in our having a large baked duck for food on a Sunday.

My mother always made baked pork with the skin done in a rich, golden, crispy crackling, and she served it with peas and rice, sweet potato, cucumber "prickle," lettuce leaves placed under slices of fresh tomatoes, and shaved, raw carrots. The green pigeon peas, picked from the trees bordering our land, were "doved," meaning they were scalded in boiling water, sprinkled with salt and black pepper, and baked.

The Demerara rice had been picked and subjected to several washings before it was steamed. Only now do I realize why we called the rice from Demerara, and later from Trinidad, "white rice." White rice was nothing more than plain rice. Through a quirk in my understanding of race and colour, I had thought that the term implied ethnicity, and that white rice was of higher quality and must have been prepared expressly for the tables of the Plantation.

Everyone in the villages where I grew up ate their Sunday meal at the same time: about one o'clock, following church, whether the service was at the Sin-Matthias Anglican Church in Sin-Matthias Village, at the Gospel Hall Church in Deighton's Village or at the Church of the Nazarene in Clapham. And it was the same meal, identical in almost every detail, in every home. The exorbitance of food was devoured with the same exuberance we had for church services and singing. Because we did not keep leftovers, since we had no means of refrigeration, and mostly because the food was so sweet, we ate it all off at one sitting.

On Monday, the exhaustion of Sunday, caused by nerves and gluttony and church — we attended matins at eleven o'clock, Sunday school at three and evensong at seven — was still lingering strong in the body and on the mind. Monday was also the first day of the ritual of washing clothes. In those times, a bundle of clothes was never washed in its entirety in one single day; it had to go through certain prescribed stages and procedures, just as a washing machine today goes through a cycle. For instance, a woman soaked her clothes on Monday in water that had no soap; washed them on Tuesday using soap and hung them on the clothes-line; rinsed them on Wednesday and hung them on the clothes-line; "blued" them and starched them on Thursday and hung them on the clothes-line; and ironed them on Friday, and sometimes Saturday as well.

To blue clothes, means simply that you put into the clothes an ingredient called blue, in order to take out lingering stains. To starch clothes, you dipped those that were to be ironed — and most clothes in those days were ironed, including handkerchiefs and men's underwear — into a home-made liquid that contained starch obtained from the root of the cassava plant. The collar of a shirt that is starched in this way, and then ironed, comes out hard as dealboard, enough to gouge the neck or burst a blood vessel.

Of course, there is an application of the term "starch" that is current in circumstances more social than the washing of clothes. When an adversary suggests that she is going to "*starch* your arse with blows," it is time for prudence. It is not the time to array your laundry on a clothes-line for her inspection. It is time to turn and run away.

I grew up with neighbours whose households contained mother, father, brother, sister, five children and, in some cases, two grandmothers and mother-in-law. The size of the washing that faced them on Monday mornings was phenomenal. But the two grandmothers and the one mother-in-law contributed to this work.

Monday, therefore, was not the best day to cook food that required a lot of time for the selection and preparation of ingreasements. Busy with washing, the woman of the house would resort to a meal of cou-cou or "dryfood," mainly because of the short time it took to prepare it.

Cou-cou is made by stirring corn meal in water in which okras have been boiled. It is served with some kind of fish — usually flying fish, if it is in season. The flying fish is on the Barbadian coat of arms. Apart from flying fish, which are sold by the dozen, we always had for our table shark, dolphin, king-fish, swordfish and other larger fish whose names only fishermen knew. These varieties were all sold by the pound; no one has ever explained this peculiarity. These kinds of fish could be bought in whole or in part. The head of most fish was the favoured part.

Fish head. What a bounty! What a delightful feast, with its various tastes, some parts reminding you of beef, some of lamb, some, naturally, of fish. And sometimes, some parts remind you of lobster, which is like gold. What a culinary microcosm of Wessindian succulence is the fish head!

Fish was always plentiful, and countless species were caught every day in the waters that surround Barbados. The kind of fish you served was to a large extent determined by the day of the week. Also taken into consideration was the social significance of the occasion, if the day and the occasion did not coincide.

Let us take dolphin, for instance. Dolphin, when boiled and cut up into pieces, was not considered "proper" to be served on Sunday. Dolphin fried, with a slight covering or batter of flour, and seasoned deeply with thyme, black pepper fresh from the tree, ginger and eschalots was, on the other hand, regarded as "fairly proper" for a Sunday table. Flying fish, when steamed or boiled, was not considered suitable for Sunday. But when fried in a batter and either buckled back (folded) or fried straight (laid out to its full length), with or without the head attached, it was a fine Sunday fare — particularly if it was the time when flying fish was scarce.

I was speaking recently to my eighty-one- to ninety-one-year-old mother about "fish pots" and the kinds of fish we used to catch in them. Barbadians had precious little regard for "pot fish" and other species — few of whose names I remember. But fish like barbaras, cavalleys, jacks and ning-nings are indescribably tasteful. When fried, they give off an aroma whose sweetness is next, so the vicar said, to the feeling of being in heaven! The vicar liked pot fish, fried and served with green pigeon peas and white rice. It was his maid, a distant cousin of my mother's, who told us that he ate his pot fish and white rice dressed only in his red cassock, with not another stitch of clothes on. "I serves him his pot fish as he like it, and *bram!* — I gone through the door!"

We either travelled into Town to buy fish from the several fish market stalls there or else we gathered on the beach at the appropriate times, mornings and evenings, and bought them straight out of the boats from the fishermen themselves.

"Fish? Fish here!" the fishermen shouted, somewhat unnecessarily.

Always in the evenings, after four o'clock, there were the voices of women walking through the villages and neighbourhoods, with heavy trays or baskets on their heads, padded for comfort and laden with freshly caught fish. "Fish? Fish here!" This was sometimes pronounced as one word. "Fish? Fish here! Come and get muh! Fish! Fish here! All-a-penny!" These women advertised their produce with shrieks, walking miles and calling out until the last fish was sold.

"All-a-penny" means, literally, all you can carry for the price of a penny. It meant also that the catch was bountiful. During these all-a-penny evenings, my mother would buy three dozen for the price of one shilling. Before I went to bed that night, the fish would be cleaned, scaled, gutted, cleaned a second time, soaked in lime juice and salt, seasoned and fried (or steamed). And my mother and I would eat them all!

Along with the fish, she would make flour-bakes — a mixture of flour, salt, sugar, nutmeg, vanilla essence and a beaten egg — and fry this mixture in butter or lard.

As for Tuesday, a day with no outstanding food associated with it, I have no sharp memory of what we ate. On a few Tuesdays my mother cooked plain rice and "friggazee" cod fish with a butter sauce. The salt fish cooked in this way, in a buck pot, was usually dry; and even with the butter sauce, the rice did not have that sticky, gluey consistency that I liked, produced by mixing it with fresh pigeon peas picked from our land.

Wednesday was my favourite day for food. On Wednesdays, the neighbourhood butcher was the chieftain.

My mother remembers that on Wednesdays the butcher "butchered-up the blasted sheep," and we always had mutton soup, with eddoes and barley.

"Mutton soup, boy! I remember to today how it taste, when I used to make it for you! Yes! Mutton soup, with eddoes — the boiling eddoes, not the pulp-eddoes whiching is for cooking with dryfood. Mutton soup with eddoes! And parts of the sheep head whiching we used to get from Mr. Whittaker. And flavoured with salt pig tail whiching we used to get from Miss Edwards's shop. You used to like your salt pig tails!"

Mutton soup cooked this way is whitened from the eddoes, which are boiled soft, so soft that they melt in the mouth. The huge chunks of mutton, with its delicious taste, not so strong as beef or pork, are enhanced by the pig tail, with its stronger saltiness. And if it was the season for reaping corn, the dumplings, which normally were made only of white flour, would now be made with an additional ingreasement, the reflection of this wondrous golden season. The addition of corn meal to flour gives the dumplings "supstance" and a tantalizing heaviness.

Yes, Wednesday was my best day for food.

Thursday coincided with the washday ritual of starching clothes, a day of hard labour, so the food was light — usually without meat, chicken, fish or peas and rice.

"You could cook *anything*" on a Thursday, my mother told me recently in a long conversation from her home in Mount Laurel, New Jersey. We were talking about Barbados in the forties.

On Friday, which we considered to be the last day of the week, the larder was running low or completely empty, and dryfood was served. Dryfood was another of my favourite foods when I was a boy. It is made from sweet potatoes, yams, eddoes and punkin, all boiled with a piece of salt beef or salted pig tail in the water to flavour the pot. For a more substantial meal, my mother would make flour dumplings with a fair amount of baking soda in them, so that they were light enough to float at the top of the pot that held the ground provisions, or ingreasements. "Dry" refers to the fact that these ingreasements were eaten without emphasis on sauce or gravy. I always had a weakness for flour dumplings and salted meats.

The scheduling of meals, when I was growing up in Barbados, was strictly determined by social status. Status went farther than money. With status, you had all that money could buy; but if you had no status in the village, you could not "trust" (buy on credit) the rice, peas and salt meat you needed for cooking your food. You might have to wait until a friend intervened or the mood of the shopkeeper changed. Until this charity was demonstrated, you couldn't "go in the galley and start your pot."

Status showed its discriminating face when there was a scarcity of foodstuffs. If you were not a woman of standing, a purse full of shillings could not guarantee you any groceries; you had to wait until the "regular" customers were served. This was the village's way of enforcing rationing. But more than this, it was a way of reminding you of your place. A woman with an unflattering lack of status was reminded of it whenever she entered the shop.

"I want three pounds of that pickle-herring I see the lorry deliver to you yesterday," she would say.

"Lord, girl!" the woman who owned the shop would tell her. "You don't know that they didn't leave *none* for me! I send in my order since last week, when I hear that a shipment coming in from Canada!"

"You ain't get none in-true?" the saddened woman would say. She would already have peeled her sweet potatoes before leaving home. And her okras would have been sliced, for making the meal-corn cou-cou. "And I don't have *anything* to eat this cou-cou I cooking with."

"None, girl. They ain't leff none! Those bastards who call themselves wholesale merchants, down in Town?" the shopkeeper moaned.

The woman would leave, dejected.

A minute later my mother would flounce into the shop. The shopkeeper, like a spy, would make sure that the previous customer was out of sight and hearing. Then, like two conspirators, they would whisper.

"*Don't* tell nobody," the shopkeeper says, looking left and right although there is no one else in the shop. "I get a few sides. But I *can't* sell piece to any-and-every Tom-Dick-and-Harry who cross these doors. No, child! I got to look after my regular customers. Put this in your basket, *quick*! Don't let anybody see."

"I didn't get none from you, you hear!" my mother says now, confirmed in conspiracy with the shopkeeper.

"Not from me! I didn't have none to sell nobody! You certainly didn't get it from this shop!"

On the way out, to cement their thickness of bond, my mother would say, "And I hear you expecting some o' those nice tins o' pilchards from up in Canada, so if . . ."

"Don't you worry, Mistress Luke," the shopkeeper says, addressing my mother by her married name. "It going be *here*. When you come. And if you don't come, and if I see the boy, he will tek it to you. Don't worry, Mistress Luke."

"Well, *all right*, then."

"*All right*."

So, we now have some historical and cultural background to Barbadian cuisine. You have travelled through a lifetime with me. You have seen the three villages — Sin-Matthias, Deighton Road and Clapham — in which I grew up. You have seen me in a mango tree "studying," memorizing Scripture for my examinations; and you have seen, with my eyes, the rows of green waving sugar cane which in my fantasies were always transformed into waves.

Water to me was never stationary. It always made me think of going someplace different from the small island in which I was born. In those days, the forties, people travelled by boat. But when I left Barbados many years later, in 1955, it was on a Trans-Canada Air Lines plane. TCA was the means of my carriage, as Bob Marley says in song. And my day-dreams about the fields of sugar cane turned into a harsher reality as we travelled over the dirtier, inhospitable green of the Atlantic Ocean in a shaking TCA plane.

I ask myself the same question that Canadians used to ask me — a question that used to make me get vex-vex: "Why would you leave a nice warm place like Barbados to come to this cold country?"

I could give one answer: "I didn't leave Barbados to come here as an immigrant. I came here to study." But I must confess that there was also an aspect of daring, of adventure, of having been stifled within the dimensions of an island. Living in an island was delightful during my childhood, but my first journey outside Barbados told me how confining an island is, and has to be.

Another answer could be that I came because of a Canadian I met in Barbados. He was a Westerner, a science teacher at the Coleridge & Parry School, where I taught English, Latin and Scripture to the Fifth, Third and First Forms, respectively. His name is Allan Welles. He wore horn-rimmed glasses with lenses as thick as those of the telescope in the observatory on Clapham Hill. It was his sense of liberalism, his sense of humour, his self-negating honesty that persuaded me to "try out this place called Canada" and see what it was like.

Fate too had a hand in my coming. In the parlance of the obeah-man, the practitioner of witchcraft in the village, there was an omen at my setting out, an omen as at the birth of kings and emperors, when the heavens and the skies and the sea churn in violent applause at the birth. The omen at my departing was a hurricane. It was named Hazel. Hazel flattened Barbados. She also flattened Toronto. The Trans-Canada Air Lines plane was therefore taking me from one destruction to another. I could still see Hazel's mood in the limbs of Toronto trees ripped by its fury, days after my arrival.

I did not bring samples of my mother's hot-cuisine in my luggage. All I brought from Barbados to make me less nostalgic in the four years I was to spend in Toronto's ice and frost, snow and winter, was a case of Mount Gay Rum. I brought no sweetbread, no sugar cakes, no buckled-back flying fish, no cassava pone — things that modern-day immigrants bring. But in my heart, in my blood and in my mind, I carried all the conversations and all the eccentricities of my mother, my aunts, cousins and grandmothers, those strong, beautiful, black, light-complexioned and white women who nurtured me, fed me from their pots, loved me and turned me into the man I am today.

I can still see those women performing feats of culinary magic, with all the arrogance, intolerance to criticism, and competitiveness that is peculiar to persons whose knowledge is based exclusively on an oral tradition, on myth and on the inheritance of customs. My mother, and all those other women who surrounded me, ignored the hot-cuisine of France, convinced that what came out of their pots, resting on three rocks placed in the shape of a triangle, was superior to anything cooked in Europe.

My memories of them, as I stood in dark, smoky kitchens watching them cooking and listening to their conversations, have now led me to share with you, in this light-hearted manner but still with some seriousness, *our* version of hot-cuisine born and bred in Barbados. Or, as my mother would say, "our ways of cooking."

Bakes

One afternoon, after school, in days of yore, as I was walking up Bishop's Court Hill with my bicycle, because the hill was too steep even for the lowest gear of my ladies'-wheel Raleigh, I was able to catch up to a big mule-drawn cart. The cart was trying to climb the same hill, transporting goods such as flour, sugar, corn meal, Rankin Biscuits, lard oil, pig tails, salted beef neck bones, salt fish from up in Newfoundland and rancid butter from Australia — taking these things from the wholesale merchants in Town to lil peddling shops all over the countryside, retailing the merchants' goods that had been sold to them at high prices and still making a lil profit themselves.

As I pondered this aspect of native economics, the poor mule-cart driver, who worked so hard — fifteen, sixteen, seventeen hours a day — and who was partly chloroformed by the stench of the mule's urine, began to fall off into a little doze. The mule, accustomed to this journey — it was all uphill for miles — soon began to fall asleep too. And then *bram!* the mule fall down. At the same time one of the cart's wheels hit a big rock in the road. *Bruggadown!* The bags o' flour fall off the cart and one split-open in the middle of the road.

The villagers heard the report, and the driver, who was on his back in the middle of the road, unable to move, start cursing the mule, the town merchants, their mothers and God, while the mule lay down in the road with his four feet cocked-up in the air.

Federation start. People began flowing out of their houses, alleys and lanes like peas spilling across a linoleum floor. The whole neighbourhood swarmed the mule cart with their bowls, plastic cups and cooking tots, and one woman, who could not find any utensil large enough to carry away the flour, resorted to using her "po," her bedpan, having first washed it out under the warm afternoon water of the public standpipe.

The men and women knew about germs and mules and the public road and public decency, so they scraped off only the good flour from the top. They swept the black flour into the gutter, and washed the road with water from the public standpipe.

The mule-cart driver then washed his face and continued on his journey. He understood the villagers. Flour was the staple of their diet, but during those starving war-days there was none, and the people had been "cutting and contriving." They had had to learn how to make an alternative from grated sweet potato and grated cassava; but it wasn't the same as their beloved Canadian flour.

Once, the Nazzis torpedoed a merchant ship, the HMS *Cornwallis*, as she lay at anchor right inside the waters of our harbour. The torpedo made the *Cornwallis* lean on its right side, and the skies became black throughout all of Barbados. The ship's secret cargo — flour — was damaged. Some went to the bottom, but some was salvaged. And the people bawled for murder — not against the Nazzis, because they almost blow-way the whole island, but against the Allieds, who had brought flour right into our harbour, right under our noses, within our reach of begging and of hunger, and were intent on shipping all of it back up to Europe, to feed the "theatres of war." So the people, loyal black Britons before the HMS *Cornwallis* entered the outer careenage of the harbour, started cussing and abusing the Allieds, and in turn hailed for the Nazzis.

Flour was usually the last thing left in your larder no matter how poor you were. So flour was the backbone of your diet, your nutrition. It was precious, like air. If you had flour in your larder, you never went hungry. You could always have bakes: flour, salt, sugar and lard oil. The cheapest meal in the world to make. Nobody can be so poor that they can't have a nice meal o' bakes.

"When you don't have a bake to fry," my mother always said, "then you know you're blasted poor. Poor as a bird's arse!"

Bakes! Basic, beautiful, black Barbadian hot-cuisine. A food of great historical significance that can be found in the lexicon of Barbadian sociology, with a strong anthropological association with the days of slavery, thereby giving bakes a most serious cultural-culinary antecedent in the life of this great little nation of Barbados!

Basically, flour and water is all you need. Well, almost. If you don't have sugar, too bad; but it's not the end of the world. If you have salt, you'll need just a pinch. And for this small expenditure of effort and money, the satisfying result of a full stomach is extraordinary.

If you is a hard-working, working-class person, you would know how to make the real ethnic or lighterman bakes, which are heavy and thick and filling. Lighters were big Venetian-like barges that uses to go out from the wharf into deep water where the ships had to anchor, to bring back the cargo of the merchant vessels that were too big to come into the shallow water of the careenage and wharf. The lightermen uses to pull the big big oars of the lighters, oars so big that it take two big men to pull one oar!

All the lightermen uses to eat bakes for lunch. Big, fat, thick bakes made from flour, sugar, salt and water, fried in lard oil. They were half an inch thick and two inches in diameter, and would "cloyd" the lighterman, meaning they uses to full up his stomach quick-quick and stay long-long. He uses to wash down these bakes with "swank." Swank is a drink made from molasses diluted with water, and with a piece of chipped ice in it, if he had ice. This lunch would give the lighterman all the strength he needed to pull them massive oars of the lighters. And as he pulled, he uses to sweat bucketsful o' perspiration.

"Pull! Pull! Pull-pull!" they would cry out, as they rounded the corner, coming full steam into the careenage, dreaming of lunch and bakes.

"Row, row, row-yuh-boat! *Pull!*" The lightermen learn that song about pulling barges through their fondness for flour bakes and from English sea shanties.

The flour that was imported into Barbados in those days came from Canada, in nice, white, cotton flour bags with the name and address of the mill that ground the flour printed in red and blue lettering. The lighterman did not throw away his flour bags. During the days of slavery and colonization, nothing was thrown away. Nothing.

The pig's ears were not thrown away. The pig maws were not buried like your navel string. The pig feet were not cast asunder. Neither was the pig's blood. Not even the pig's bladder. Small boys blew their breaths into the pig's bladder, till their eyes got big and red from the pressure and the bladder was on the verge of bursting, at which point they twisted its neck, tied it and made it into a football and pretended they were beating the English six-nil in a Cup Final at Wembley Stadium in London!

So, too, with the flour bags. Cotton was the best thing to wear next to the skin in the hot sun, and the bags were regarded as nice dress material for the poor. Before they were sewn into shirts, short pants, skirts, aprons, sliders for men and bloomers for women, they were bleached. If in those days you looked into any backyard in any poor neighbourhood, you would see some rock-stones arranged on the ground, in a group, and on those stones you would see flour bags spread out, bleaching in the sun.

The bags were washed by using a lot of blue, a lot of white-head bush, and a lot of blue soap imported from Away. For days and days, patient as the sun travelling through the blue skies, women would put these flour bags through the bleaching and washing process many times, until they turned into a miraculous snowy white.

What a sight! What a wonder! Pure white. Almost like the sea-island cotton from St. Vincent, only thing, these flour bags had no silk in them.

If you were watching a cricket game and your eyes were good, you would often spot a small speck of blue, as large as a comma or a period, on a player's shirt. And you would immediately recognize that the shirt was made from a flour bag. All that bleaching and blueing and the rays of the hot sun had failed to obliterate *all* the letters. That spot, that lingering fraction, perhaps part of the letter *C* in the word *Canada*, would be all it took to stamp this young,

ambitious cricketer with the poorness of his social origins.
Any prowess he demonstrated that Saturday afternoon on
the playing field, the flash of his bat in a cover drive, like
Frank Worrell, would be second in significance to the fact
that he was "discovered," during his début with the First
Eleven team, to be dressed, turned out, in a flour-bag shirt!

The flour bag and the game of cricket — that English
pastime symbolizing order, class, fairness and Empire,
played by the aristocracy of the colony, of the dominion,
and of the Mother Country — certainly did *not* go together!
Blame would rest at the door and in the washtub of the poor
cricketer's mother. And the cricketer would suffer the teasing and the many reminders of class and poverty for years
and years afterwards, until he was welcomed into his grave.

"Boy, you are wearing flour bag!"

The condemnation of this insult was as loud as the
voice of the speaker.

"A flour-bag shirt to Sunday School? You poor as a
bird's arse, boy!"

This statement of salutation could, and did, define a
man's sartorial unsophistication; and it marked him for life.

Today, in these times of harking back to and clutching
at one's cultural roots, you see young people wearing flour-
bag shirts or skirts — especially during the carnival season in Barbados, in London, England, in Brooklyn up in
Amurca, and in Toronto during Caribana. And this festive
attire proudly bears the brand name, the name of the mill
and the country of manufacture in bold colours in the most

conspicuous locations, such as the chest. Nowadays, this is style, a proclamation of pride in national ethnicity.

And the same thing with bakes. I remember some students who took bakes to school for their luncheon. They were easily detected as bakes-eaters because the grease from the lard oil in the bakes would always leak through the brown paper bag that held them. The poor boys' social status would be exposed and shame brought upon their heads and upon their families' circumstances.

Nowadays you can make bakes with an easy, bold heart, and invite the high and the mighty in society to dine with you, to show them that you know and love your culture. So now I'm going to tell you how to turn ordinary flour into a marvellous meal of bakes.

You can cook bakes even on a Sunday if you have nothing else to cook, although bakes are usually eaten on a Friday, when almost all the things in your larder are gone.

To think of having to cook bakes on a Sunday, the day when you are supposed to have the best meal of the week! But don't mind, things are hard with everybody. The economic situation is bad, jobs scarce, and the government not making things any more better for people. People unemployed. When you are hungry and poor, it doesn't matter what kind o' food you eat on a particular day, so long as it is food and it taste sweet.

These bakes that I'm going to tell you how to make are bakes that middle- and upper-middle-class Barbadian people does make. With bakes, so too with everything. Food has always been tied up with social status and historical protocol. A middle-class person would add in certain other ingreasements with the flour, salt, sugar and water to reflect her status in society. The better the ingreasements you have in your bakes, the higher those ingreasements can lift you, even beyond the class to which you already belong; and they will make your bakes turn out lighter, too. Complexion of skin and social status, and the lightness of bakes, go hand in hand.

You'll need a large bowl, plain, ordinary white flour, a touch o' salt, a tablespoon o' white sugar, a touch o' baking powder, a fresh nutmeg to grate off a few grains, a wedge o' butter, one or two drops o' vanilla essence, an egg beaten up with a fork, some water and some lard oil, or lard, or cooking oil — *not* olive oil.

Pour about half a pound o' flour into the bowl. Flour, notwithstanding the snobbery of class, is still the backbone. Flour does not change. Not unless you buy your flour in countries that are members of the Gee-Sevens economic club. If you buy your flour in First World countries, it won't have weebulls in it. But if you are of the Third or Fourth Worlds, in a place like Barbados, the weebulls in your flour will also be in the flour of the Governor General and the Chief Justice. Your flour and their flour will be in the same shipment that came from Away, and that is held in the bonds in Town. Flour that is left to stand too long in these bonds attracts weebulls and ants and mice. So arm thyself with a fine-meshed sieve!

Sprinkle a lil salt into the flour, then the white sugar. Throw in a touch o' baking powder and grate off a few grains o' nutmeg. Mix up these ingreasements; and when they mix in good, add in a wedge o' butter. Drop one or two drops o' vanilla essence on the flour, and after you beat-up the egg, pour it over the flour mixture.

Start stirring. Stir until everything mix in good. Whilst you are mixing up the batter for your bakes, you could always spend your time dreaming that you are in a more better social class, with the financial position to go along with it, to be able to cook something like bake chicken, or even a fry pork chop on a blessed Sunday like today. But humble as they are, bakes are still the groundsill of dietary happiness. If you don't have a penny in your pocket, you can still thank God, 'cause you have flour.

Now, you have the water in a glass; you don't need no measuring cup. You'll need enough water to make the batter smooth, but not too watery or too stiff as if you're making dough for bread. Pour the water evenly over the flour mixture and stir with a pot spoon. But supposing you don't have any baking powder? You can use club soda instead of plain water, 'cause you want bubbles in your bakes, to make them light, man!

When your batter smooth, get a frying pan and pour in some lard oil or lard or cooking oil until it almost cover the bottom of the pan. Now, the thing to watch is this: make sure the element on your stove even, or flat, or level. Adjust the frying pan to suit. To test that the frying pan ready, all you got to do is to hold the back o' your hand *over* the pan — not inside the hot oil! — and you can test the hotness. When the oil get hot, but not hot enough to burn up the bakes, gently drop tablespoons o' batter in that frying pan. And the minute you drop in enough tablespoonfuls to cover the bottom of the pan, get your fork and put it underneath each bake, to prevent it from sticking.

When the edges start getting fried, you know it's time to turn each and every bake over, on the next side. And that is all it take to make bakes.

But still you might wonder: "What more can I do to make these bakes taste less like real bakes and more like pancakes? I hear that people up in Europe and North Amurca, in places like Brooklyn and New York City and Toronto, does-eat bakes that look like pancakes. Perhaps, if I can get these bakes light and fluffy like those Aunt Jemima pancakes, I could christen my bakes by another name, and call them 'fries' or 'floats'!"

You are not making bakes any more. You are talking about fries, if you please. High-class bakes. So fry them not in lard oil, but in butter. You could even use the thick, yellow, rancid butter imported from Australia. High-class bakes are thin, and yellowish in colour because of the egg, and light as a feather — too light to full-up the stomach of a lighterman and help him pull those oars!

If you are in possession of only a little flour, a little salt and a little lard oil, which could even be white lard melted down, you can only dream of having fries. These ingreasements can't make bakes of middle-class lightness.

Now, what are you going to serve with your bakes? The culturally traditional accompaniment is salt fish. Roasted salt fish. Salt fish with the skin still on it and the bones still in. But if things with you are not too grim, and you are indeed a member of the middle class, you could soak the salt fish in water overnight, take out the bones, and "sawtay" the salt fish in a saucepan with some butter, onions and a sliced tomato, and serve this with the bakes.

Ironically, and as every Barbadian knows, bakes taste more sweeter a few hours after they're fried, when they are cold; and better still when they are left over till the next day. The oil and the sugar and the flour would have had time to work on one another and "co-aggillate," so that when you bite into one, you will hear a clicking sound. And this is the sign for you to close your two eyes and don't open them until the bake is finished off, completely eaten.

But who in the whole of Barbados, in their right mind, with nothing more to cook but flour and lard oil on a sacred day like Sunday, would leave the bakes for the next day, merely because they taste more sweeter when cold? And cause yourself to expire from hunger, on a blessed Sunday?

Privilege

"Mr. Clarke, do you know what 'privilege' is?" It was seven o'clock on a Friday evening, and the voice on the other end of the telephone was that of the prime minister of Barbados, the Right Honourable Errol Walton Barrow, PC. I was his adviser on internal political affairs.

Whenever he addressed me as "Mr. Clarke" instead of "Austin" or "Tom," I knew immediately that I was in serious political trouble. But on this Friday evening I could not think of my transgression. Perhaps I had given him the wrong advice about broadcasting or some other matter of national importance.

"Privilege, sir," I began uncertainly, "is . . . ahm . . . a right, sir. Or an advantage. Privilege, Prime Minister, could be an immunity granted to a person, or to a class, or . . ."

"Austin," his booming voice came through the telephone, but in a more jocular tone and with some amusement in it, "not *that* kind o' privilege! I mean *real* privilege."

Real privilege?

While recognizing his less formal manner of addressing me, I began to stammer some more. He had gone from "Mr. Clarke" to "Austin" in one telephone call, and it made me even more nervous.

I continued searching my brain, in the stifling air around me, for the definition of "privilege" that I thought was the correct one, or the one he wanted, or the one he would accept.

"Tom," he said, now jovial and amused at my expense, "you mean to tell me that a former professor at Yale University and at other Amurcan Ivy League universities, teaching people Black Studies and Black Culture, and coming down here getting-on like a black intellectual, *doesn't know* what 'privilege' is?"

"Well, Prime Minister, 'privilege' could be when someone . . ."

"Get your chauffeur to drive you down here to Kampala, right now!"

It was an order. I had to get to Kampala, his private residence, on the dot!

"And I shall show you real 'privilege'!" the Prime

Minister added. But there was no need for this tautology. Then he put the phone down.

The journey to Kampala took me from my house in Paradise Heights, down the hill, opposite the iron gates of the Cave Hill campus of the University of the West Indies. There we made a left turn, travelled along the frangipani hedge of Paradise Beach Hotel, which was popular with tourisses down from Canada and Amurca for sun and sin, and drove farther down a short driveway cluttered with fragrant flowers.

As I walked up the two or three coral stone steps to the front door of Kampala, a uniformed policeman shuffled to attention. I paid no regard to his half-hearted salute and casual manner.

"Clarkey, boy?" he said. "How?"

I was worried that he knew the circumstances of my arrival. I was about to face the Prime Minister, who was going to show me "real privilege." My knowledge of Barbadian language, with all its diplomatic nuances of ambivalence, *double entendre* and duplicity, prompted me in my frantic moment of arrival to interpret the Prime Minister's words to mean that he was about to strip me of my rank, take away my diplomatic passport and privilege, and show me the real power of a prime minister, the girth of *his* privilege.

Members of the Cabinet were there, drinking Scotch and soda, Mount Gay Rum and ginger ale, and Gordon's Gin and Kola tonic. They were laughing, probably because the Prime Minister had already told them that I did not know what privilege was.

When I walked into the drawing room and saw all those powerful men sitting down, some sprawled on couches and chairs, I grew even more frightened. The Prime Minister had summoned me to his austere presence to be bawled out in front of all these Cabinets.

The minister of foreign affairs, a powerful barrister-at-law of five foot three who went to Oxford for Law and Torts and to Columbia to do more Law and more Torts, was telling the deputy prime minister, "Man, I drive a hard seed in the minister o' trade' clothes last Friday night, when we was playing dominoes up by Phillip!"

The deputy prime minister was a man who went to Codrington College in Barbados to study theology. He didn't like the Bible, though, as much as he liked Livy and Caesar's *Gallic Wars*, so he exchanged Codrington for Durham up in England, and read Law and Contracts after Classical Studies.

"Man, the minister o' trade? He learn his dominoes in Amurca. Not here! Not in Barbados! It was a sweet six-love we poured in his seat, last Friday night!"

And the minister of trade, a tall, handsome fellow, who had left Barbados for Amurca, went to Columbia University to study politics and philosophy, and came back with three or four degrees behind his name, replied, "Bullshit!" He had stopped talking like a Barbadian and had started talking like a Yankee, an African Amurcan from Harlem.

I held my two hands to my mouth in astonishment, wonder and shock to hear how ministers of trade address ministers of foreign affairs and deputy prime ministers. My God in heaven!

"Bullshit!" the African Amurcan from Barbados exclaimed again, as if they hadn't heard him the first time. "The two o' you? The two o' you's acolytes when it come to dominoes! Ask the attorney-general sitting-down beside me! Ask him. Ask him! Who share licks last Friday night?"

Lord have his mercy! Calling on the chief law officer, the Lord High Chancellor? A man learned in *all* the laws of torts, contracts, and criminal and civic jurisprudence? A man who received his higher education at Cambridge University and came back down to Barbados with LL B, LL M, LL D and D Litt.? And to be addressed so?

And then the Prime Minister came in.

No one heard his entry; he walked slow and quiet like a cat stalking a mouse. When I saw him, I started to tremble. But the Cabinets and the privy counsellors started laughing in union, like the way they vote in parliament in the House of Assembly.

"Look he here!" the Prime Minister said.

The Cabinets started laughing louder. "Kee-kee-kee! Ohhh, kee-kee-kee! Look at him!"

"Let me show you, Austin," the Prime Minister said, "real privilege."

And then the Prime Minister, with his own two hands, gave me my first plate of Privilege.

"Look at the big professor from a Ivy League university up in Amurca, who doesn't know what privilege is! You see what happens to our biggest brains when they leave here, to go Away to North Amurca and learn a lot o' foolishness? And then come back here and forget their roots?" the Prime Minister was appealing to the Cabinets.

"Yes, Prime Minister," I said.

"Tom," he then said, "Privilege is slave food, man. I just cooked this. We're having Privilege for dinner."

"But do you know what to do with that?" the attorney-general said to me, and laughed some more, and louder. The Cabinets joined him.

"He worse than me," the minister of trade said. "He loss his cultural roots *completely*!"

The plate was shaking in my two hands, the fork knocking against the plate.

The white rice was cooked with every grain discernible and easy to count. The okras were fresh and green and slimy, and the pieces of pig tail and salt beef were like jewels — diamonds shining through a piece of land in South Africa. When I was able to get the first forkful to my two lips and tasted it, Lord have his mercy, it went down smooth, smooth, smooth, slippery like raw oysters. And everybody stopped laughing and smiled. I ate three helpings.

And when I left their presence at about two o'clock in the morning, and my chauffeur was taking me back up the hill, all I was thinking of were the four sweetest things in the world: love, sweet food, power and Privilege.

Since it is Privilege we are talking about, the way of cooking it has to be narrated in the native language of the people who invented it: the Bajan language. But before we get
involved in this, we have to know something about the
cultural and historical origins of this meal.

Barbadians have always known that the food we eat is
"slave food," based on leavings or left-overs, the remnants
of the better cuts of meat eaten by the Plantation owners.
The Amurcans would call it soul food, but I would argue
that we Wessindians, and Barbadians in particular, had
come to soul food long before African Amurcans, African
Canadians and Africadians.

Slave food is an older concept of black aesthetics and
black culture than is soul food. We was eating it before the
1960s, when Amurcans discovered that they was no longer
"coloured" or "Negro," but was black and beautiful and
interested in African culture. We had known for a long
time that we was beautiful, although we didn't know or
care one damn that we was black. We knew that the food
we was eating was different from the food on the tables of
the Plantation people and the powerful black people, who
ate as if they was living on a Plantation themselves; but
their food was never as sweet as ours. We didn't consider
our food to be cultural or political, nor did we think of it
as hot-cuisine. Slave food doesn't have a damn thing to do
with the soul or with "black is beautiful." It has *everything*
to do with the belly.

In days of yore, your belly was usually sticking to your back, through hunger. Slaves was always hungry. Food was always scarce. They had to learn how to "cut and contrive," how to improvise. During the time of the harshest lash of slavery, and even after slavery was abolish, people had to work from sun-up till sun-down in the fields of the Plantation, planting sweet potatoes and yams, hoeing the eddoes and cutting sugar cane. And even though these people were poorer than dirt, they would still have a two-by-two parcel of land behind the chattel house that they rented from the Plantation. On this little two-by-two they started to plant a kitchen garden; and they would have dropped a few okra seeds in the ground. And after a little rain, *bram!* an okra tree spring up.

Okras is the first ingreasement you need for making Privilege, after white rice. You'll need a handful o' okras that you pick offa the tree in the backyard, or that you borrow from somebody, or that you buy in a supermarket.

Some people does slice the okras, in cartwheels. Some people does cut the okras lengthwise into two. Some people does do both. Some people does cut them up in three or four pieces. Some does put in the okras whole.

When you choosing okras in a supermarket, make sure that the okras are fresh. All you have to do is break off a little piece from the top of the okra, and if it snap off clean, the okra fresh. Buy it.

You could eat fresh okras raw, in case you want to know. As little children growing up in Barbados, long after slavery, we uses to eat okras raw, right off the tree, and sprinkled with salt. Disregard the little bristles o' hair that you does see on okras, and crunch them in your mouth.

The next ingreasement you need is rice, but Barbados didn't grow no rice. Barbados in those days didn't have no Indian population from Asia. They had a few "Indians," but these were Amerindians, the indigenous people of Barbados. And there wasn't any flat land that was swampy — nor is there to this day. So, without Indians and swampy land, Barbados could never grow rice. Rice had to come from Trinidad or Demerara, and it had to be picked.

In these modern times, you don't have to pick rice; modern-day rice is clean. But you should always wash rice in cold water, even if you buy it from a supermarket, in a plastic package that is sealed.

In colonial times, which followed the days of slavery, practically all the food we uses to eat had to come from Away — from England, Canada and Australia. Since colonized people was considered second-class to the people from Away, the food was also second-class, or of an inferior quality. Some of it, like the meat, had to be cured in brine. You would have to salt down your own pig tails and inferior cuts of beef in a barrel of brine, and leave them to settle and season for a few days before they turn into tasty meats that could be used for making Privilege.

Nowadays, you can buy pig tails and salt beef by the bucketful, already season-up and soak-down in brine, in any grocery store or supermarket. If you are in the Kensington Market in Toronto or the Brooklyn Market in New York, and you want a really nice piece o' pig tail or a sweet cut o' salt beef, you have to roll up your two shirtsleeves, up to your two elbows, take off your wristwatch and the silver bracelets, and put your two hands down deep inside that brine-barrel.

I see with my two eyes the Prime Minister of Barbados, the Right Honourable Errol Walton Barrow, PC, in the presence of the late Sir Cameron Tudor, Barbados High Commissioner to Canada, with their own two hands twirl-round the pig tails and the salt beef pieces inside a big-big white plastic pail, down in the Kensington Market, selecting the sweetest, before they would buy one single piece. So, if such powerful dignitaries could do it, who you is that you can't dip your two hands inside a brine-barrel? Do it and you will feel the nice clutching sensation of the brine, tingling through your pores and tightening up the veins of your two hands.

You have to put your hand in a brine-barrel before you come telling decent people that you have chosen the best piece o' pig tail or the sweetest cut o' salt beef. The best pig tails is the ones with skin and some fat on them, and that are thick and juicy. The best salt beef have-on bones, a little fat, and meat that is pinkish.

When you get home from the market, wash off the pig tails and the salt beef in cold water. To take out the excess salt more easily, and if you got time, leave them soaking in fresh water overnight. Another way of taking out the excess salt is to boil them. Put them in a saucepan, cover them with cold water and bring them to a boil. Pour off the water, refill the saucepan with cold water and boil them a second time. Taste the water at the second boiling and it will tell you if you have boil-out enough salt or if you need to boil them a third time.

When the pig tails and salt beef retain just the right amount o' saltiness to your taste, and just before they are soft-soft and fully cooked, put them in a frying pan with a lot o' slice-onions, fresh thyme, a few cloves o' garlic, and some oil or butter. But since we are presenting this way of cooking as a particular aspect of slave food, there ain't nothing wrong with using lard, or ordinary, cheap lard oil. If you have nothing but olive oil in your larder, use it, nuh! It can't kill yuh.

One thing about cooking that comes from the slave days is that you have to feel-up everything and put your two hands in everything and on everything that you are cooking. You have to touch-up the food and love-up the food. Rub your two hands over the pig tails and the salt beef, together with the seasoning. If you do not touch-up and love-up the meats and the ingreasements, your food is not going-respond and taste sweet when it done.

Put the pig tails and salt beef over a hot fire and stir a little. The thing is to seal the skin, not to fry the pig tails till they are cooked.

Place the okras that are cut up in a pot with cold water and put them on a medium heat. When the water start boiling, drop in the pig tails and the salt beef. You don't need no salt. But add a little fresh hot pepper.

When the pig tails and salt beef are almost soft enough to eat, put in your rice and bring the water to a boil. The minute she boil, turn she down. And stir she, from the bottom. You might have to stir she, now and then, from time to time, to make sure that with the pig tail and the salt beef in the same pot, she don't stick to the bottom of the pot.

When the rice done — and you will know that she done, because the rice grains are now cooked dry and they soft, and you can still count every rice grain — you going see lovely pieces o' half-pink meats and shades o' green from the okras and the pink of the okra seeds mixed up in the rice.

Oh my God! When you survey the contents of that pot, after you have taken off the lid and open-she-up, such a waft of historical and cultural goodness going blow in your face! Such a strong reminder from the slave days, such a powerful smell of Barbadian hot-cuisine, is going to greet you that your mouth is bound to spring water and salivate, in a contemporaneous salvation of salivation.

"Why couldn't I have been a slave too?" You are bound to axe yourself this question. "Why did they have to abolish slavery before I learn how to cook Privilege?" But this is just idle, overenthusiastic thinking and talk. All you doing is fantasizing, wishing you could eat this nice, good-good food, day in day out, instead of only once in a blue-moon, when a prime minister cook it for you.

Privilege, like other kinds o' slave food, was the back-bone of existence for we. It was consumed regularly all over Barbados, and the people didn't even know they was eating Privilege!

It was only when things got better, politically, financially and socially, and when cultural awareness improved during the sixties, that Privilege was accepted as a dish that you would have the gall to serve at a party. If you was an artist or an intellectual, you would serve it to impress people that you remember your cultural roots.

Before you serve Privilege, remember to stir-she-up and make sure that everybody get at least one piece o' pig tail and one piece o' salt beef in their plate, along with the okras and the rice. Siddown with a Heineken beer or a Mount Gay rum mixed with Coke, and iam-off this nice "bittle" in the company of Cabinet ministers and the politically almighty — or just with ordinary friends.

Dryfood

You are really scraping the bottom of the barrel when you have to cook dryfood. When your larder real empty, and no meat is to be found anywhere in your house, not even a piece o' salt fish, which we call cod, or a tin o' Fray Bentos corn beef, or sardines from Norway and Newfoundland, or pilchards, fish that does come in a tin from up in England and isn't caught in the waters o' Barbados, or tin-salmon, which is very expensive because it have to be imported from up in Canada, you can still cook dryfood — although you are getting close to vegetarianism.

In my mother's book, a vegetarian is somebody who is not concern with his or her diet and health. "Someone who prefer bush and grass, as if they is sheeps and cows, is somebody who don't have enough food to put in his mouth," she always say.

Only vegetarians eat dryfood regularly — and like to eat it, too. It is not considered normal for a person to cook food that doesn't have some amount o' meat or fish to go with it. Only someone who is starving, who don't have the money to buy a fish head or a single flying fish or even the head of a dolphin — in other words, a person who is "catching his arse" — has to eat dryfood. A person at this stage is a person one remove from having to cook bakes for breakfast, lunch and dinner.

But dryfood is also prevalent in the country districts where there are Plantations and farms, where people grow their own food. Dryfood is made with ground provisions, or "breadkind" as my mother calls them, such as sweet potatoes, eddoes (which become slimy when you boil them to make them more easier to slide down your throat), soft yellow punkin (or pumpkin, as it is known in better society), breadfruit that has been boiled and sliced, squash, and christophenes, which are good for the belly and for normalties (meaning that it is a purgative) and even better for you when you're "suffering from pressure," meaning that you have high blood pressure.

Dryfood originated with the slaves and, historically speaking, the procuring or collection of the ground provisions was an adventure, an exercise in piracy, a midnight bivouac, a secret mission behind enemy lines. Penetrating enemy lines in peacetime was nothing more than stealing from the Plantation.

In Clapham, most of the people were poor. "Poor as a bird's arse!" as my mother would say. "Poor, but proud, nevertheless!" And most of them used to work as "hands," or labourers, in the fields of the Wildey Plantation, which was one hundred yards from the nearest chattel house in Clapham. If you saw this Plantation, you would think, "What a lovely place!" It was as pretty as a postcard, with fields o' sugar cane stretching to the horizon and beyond the power of your eyes to see, and a lovely white road made outta marl and gravel.

The Plantation was a pristine panorama of English pastoral beauty, with its fields o' sweet potatoes, yams, big red tomatoes, sweet cassava, "poison" cassava, plantains as plentiful as the bananas that were themselves bountiful, figs and two kinds of eddoes: the ones for making soup and the ones for bare boiling and serving with dryfood. To behold these fields from a distance while passing in a car or on a bicycle was beyond belief, a vista not easily put into words.

But you should fall on your two knees and thank God that you never had to be a labourer in the fields of Wildey Plantation! When I tell you *work*? Work to kill you! And Wildey was one of the more benevolent Plantations.

The attitude of the field hands who used to work in Wildey's was similar to that of the fifth-columnist in the war. They saw the Plantation as the enemy. The Plantation had all this food, all this breadkind, and the field hands had none. So the hands helped the Plantation out with the excess food — by stealing it.

So, if you ever happen to cross the main road in Wildey's Village just before midnight on any Friday night, the night of thieves, you might see a man coming out o' the shadows near the public standpipe. And if the darkness isn't too thick, you would see something in his hand: a large, brown crocus bag. The night-watchman of the Plantation is the only man who does legitimately walk with a crocus bag in his hand — in daylight or at night. But sometimes it is the watchman himself who does do the biggest thiefing; and every other Friday-night thief, heading for the Plantation fields, does have to contend with him. The unwritten law amongst thieves is don't take any ground provisions or foodstuffs that the watchman has set aside for himself.

Thieves of my village were usually men, although some of the best thieves were women. Stealing ground provisions from the Plantation wasn't simple. You didn't just go into a field, dig up the ground provisions and then head for home. Oh no! A thief worth his salt would have to know a day or two beforehand — because most Friday nights of thiefing was usually dark-dark-dark — the exact lay of the land.

In Wildey Plantation there weren't no signs, as in housing developments in the suburbs, to tell you where you standing or hiding. There were no big, reflecting, white block letters announcing "FIELD NO. 1, WHICH CONTAINS SWEET POTATOES THAT RIPE" or "FIELD NO. 2, CONTAINING EDDOES." And a sweet potato is not just a sweet potato, like a carrot is a carrot or a rose is a rose is a rose. Oh no! Some sweet potatoes are "six weeks potatoes," some are "eight weeks," and so on.

Only through scientific calculation, intimate knowledge of Plantations and innate instincts honed over generations could a thief become successful at his profession of stealing ground provisions. He first have to pay attention to the inches of rain that had fall, and to the way that the sun had shine on a particular field between six and eleven in the morning and from two until six in the afternoon. Only with this knowledge would a thief be able to tell, even in the darkest night, which field was suitable for stealing sweet potatoes from, and which eddoes from.

If you yourself was not a field hand on the Plantation, you couldn't expect any assistance or mercy from your next-door neighbour who was one. He certainly wasn't gonna give you the layout, the dimensions, the geography, the environmental ins and outs of the particular field you had in mind to dig up. Oh no! Nor was he going to help you avoid straying a little off course in the surrounding darkness and putting your hand in a mongoose trap. Your neighbour in Wildey was not the kind o' person to want you to have a bellyful while he starved. So he would watch your movements and, through crab-in-the-bucket jealousy, be the first to give-you-way. So you also had to know the ways of other thieves before you dared to make your first move.

Now you're ready to crawl on your belly in the Plantation field with your crocus bag in hand, as if you is a real insurgent. Making your moves in the darkness o' night on a Friday night. But before your hand touch the first leaf, you have to hold your two ears to the ground and listen for the footsteps of the night-watchman. And you have to watch, in the changing darkness of midnight, for a blacker blackness that would indicate the presence of the black jacket that all night-watchmen wear to avoid detection by a thief.

After you spend all night in the darkness, digging up a field, you discover that you have made just a lil mistake in the calculations of your thiefing.

"Oh shite! I was digging up young cane-shoots, man. All the time thinking that I was in a field digging up sweet potatoes!"

You was digging up young sugar-cane plants. You can't even boil young cane-shoots to make a cup of tea! Where was the field that really have-in the sweet potatoes, that you know are fully grown and ripe with red skin and such sweet taste?

Suddenly you hear the shout, and you know that your labour as a thief has been in vain.

Blam-blam, blam!

Shots from a gun loaded with coarse-salt are fired from the hand of the manager, at close range. The pellets bring you luck — they could've been real bullets slamm' against your two balls. But you'll have to carry this testimony for the rest of your life. Everybody in Wildey Village, including your children, will know your damn business forever after.

A thief who makes this kind o' mistake is the laughing stock of the entire village and of all the villages surrounding Wildey for miles and miles. Perhaps throughout Barbados.

"Be-Christ, he gone in the people Plantation, one Friday night, to steal potatoes, and mistake young sugar-cane shoots for six-weeks. Man, he deserve more coar-salt in his arse, for making that fundamental mistake!"

"Man, good Christ in heaven! He couldn't even tell the difference between red-skin sweet potatoes and sugar-cane shoots? Don't he know that cane-shoots don't grow leaves? And he can't tell directions in the dark, neither? Wha' kind o' thief he is, then?"

And the men in Wildey Village will, from this fateful day, nickname him Mr. Sweet Potato — "Sweets" for short — and he will have to answer to this name for the rest of his life.

So stealing sweet potatoes from the Plantation fields is a serious thing. 'Cause if you slip and make a lil mistake, you'll be walking through the village for the rest of your life just like Sweets — shot in the testicles!

Sweets was not a singular case. Many other men bore physical evidence of blundering inefficiency following unsuccessful exploits in the Plantation's potato fields or chicken coops. Sometimes a sweet-potato thief would, in his exuberance to break all previous records, attempt to carry too heavy a load in one trip and end up rupturing a part of his body — usually around the groin — in the process. And when the swelling became visible and prominent, and would be seen in the bulge in his trousers, he would be dubbed with the nickname "Goadies."

But let's get down to brass tacks and cook some dryfood.

First, you got to understand that, historically, the entire meal of dryfood was cooked in one pot. People in them days had only one pot, and everything had to be cooked in that one pot. To perform this culinary miracle, women (the cooks, mainly, in them days) had to be proficient in agriculture, knowing which ground provision, for instance, the cassava or the yams, needed to be cooked longer than the sweet potatoes. They had to know what to put in first: the cassava, then the yams, then the sweet potatoes, and so on, down the line, until the ground provision that took the longest to be cooked and the ground provision that took the shortest were cooked to the same identical softness and texture.

Nowadays, of course, people have more than one saucepan to cook in. "More than one pot to pee in," as my mother says. "Things improve, boy!" Some people think that the more saucepans and pots they have, the better the things they cook are going come out. It ain't necessarily so. But in cooking this meal you may use more than one, if you have saucepans and pots to burn.

I would put in the cassava first — but make sure that it's *sweet* cassava, with thick, brown skin. Use a knife to cut off the peel and then wash she off. Put she in a pot of cold water and start she to boil.

The trick to cooking breadkind is to find some salt beef or a piece o' pig tail to put in the pot to give it flavour. So, add the salt meat along with the cassava. (The salt beef and the pig tail should be soaked overnight, or boiled first, to take out the salt from them.) Being a cook that know what you doing, you know without me telling you that you don't need to add salt, because the salt beef or pig tail already contain enough.

Now the yam. Peel the yam and cut she up in pieces to suit your taste. When the cassava been boiling for a time, add the yam. Peel the sweet potatoes, and add them to the pot after the yam been boiling for a time.

Punkin is the quickest thing to cook. After you peel off the punkin skin and slice-she-up in suitable pieces, put she in the saucepan over a low to medium heat.

Now you got time to make your flour drops. Put some flour in a bowl along with a lil salt, a lil white grannilated sugar and a dash o' baking powder, to keep them light. Add in a lil water and stir she round until she reach a certain thickness. Depending on how you feel, you could add in a lil vanilla essence or some nutmeg. But yuh don't really need these ingreasements. After all, um is only dryfood that you cooking, something that is quick to cook, something that is heavy in your belly when you eat it, something that will stop a hole.

Bring the saucepan with the breadkind to an easy boil. Scoop the flour-drop dough into lil balls with a big pot spoon, and drop them in the pot with the other members of the "dryfood brigate," as my mother calls them.

The dumplings will rise to the top and be light and nice. When all the breadkind are cooked to your liking, drain off all the water good good.

You'll want something more, like a sauce, to make this dryfood go down good and have a sweet taste. Take out the salt beef or the piece o' pig tail from the saucepan of bread-kind, and put it in a skillet with butter — if you have — and lil green onions or ordinary onions — if you have — and stir, on a low fire. You are now making a butter sauce, one of the sweetest, cheapest and easiest sauces in the world to make. Yuh don't even have to add no salt, 'cause the salt beef or pig tail would retain enough.

Now you ready to start to serve.

Each plate should represent each and every species of breadkind from the pot, with a slice o' this, a slice o' that and a flour drop or two. Pour butter sauce evenly all over each plate of dryfood.

When you are able to cut a lil pig tail, a piece o' sweet potato and a eddoe, and place all o' them in the same spoonful (or 'pon a fork if you are fussy and making a statement with knife-and-fork), the mixture of these different tastes

. . . Lord have His mercy! And when your teeth go through a flour drop and you hear that "click!", you will have your first realization of spiritual unctuousness and grace. You will know you're approaching heaven. And you'll know what sweet food those slaves in Barbados, back in bygone days, uses to cook.

Now you and me know what Sweets had-miss, when he made that little slip, stealing sweet potatoes from the Plantation. Wouldn't you, outta the goodness of your Christian conscience, pray that Sweets had come to a more better end, when he tried his hand at stealing the Plantation sweet potatoes, and came up with only young sugarcane blades?

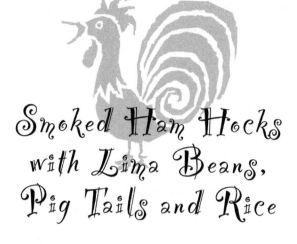

Smoked Ham Hocks with Lima Beans, Pig Tails and Rice

This is a dish that come all the way from the days of hardships and economic grief, when ingreasements were scarce and hard to procure, when the larder was almost always empty. But you still had mouths to feed. And you had to find a way, and put into action the philosophy, "Where there's a will, there's a way."

Imagine a poor woman coming home from the Plantation, dressed in white that is now tarnished grey from the rigours of her labour and from the blackness of the rich soil in the unending sugar-cane fields. She wears her dress, for prudence, down to her calves, and beneath her dress are many petticoats. She also wears an apron. Her hands and arms have suffered cuts from the sharp blades of the young sugar-cane plants she has been weeding, and her bare feet are sore and blistered from hitting the hard "cane-breaks," the narrow lanes of marl and stone she has to walk on to get from one field to another.

The end of her workday depends on whether it's the season for planting or for reaping or for manuring; and depending on whether it's potato-planting time or yam-planting time or weeding time. Some days she may be let out from the Plantation fields by the three o'clock bell. But today it is after five o'clock. Whatever the season, she is always dead tired.

She comes, black and slow and tired, through the green sea of sugar cane on her way home, and as she walks, she asks herself this question: "What I going to put on the fire this evening, to cook, eh, Lord?"

She comes across some dried cane in the gutters at the side of the fields and at the side of the road; and, economical by nature and gripped by a mixture of pragmatism and improvisation, she gathers and bundles these up to use as fuel for her fire. She carries them home on her head, which is tied with a white cloth, a remnant from an old dress, now made into a pad. During the long days in the hot sun, the pad relieves some of the weight — a basket of yams or sweet potatoes, a bunch of canes — that she must carry on her head from the field to the waiting lorry, yards away and purring like a monster anxious to leave.

She crosses from the Public Road, the main road — she calls it the "front road" — and enters the short lane leading to her house. She first stops at the village shop, where she purchases a little lard oil, a little butter and a piece of salt meat — neck bones from a cow grown and killed in a place beyond her comprehension and sense of geography, or pig tails pickled in a barrel of brine. And she might buy a little salt fish. In exchange for the rum made from sugar cane and from her labour in the sugar-cane fields, people in Canada send back this thin, white-scabbed, scabrous salt fish to Barbados. Canada also sends her Palmolive soap for washing her tired limbs, and apples — but she is too poor to purchase one of these nice English apples.

Since she has no money, she gets the shopkeeper to "trust" her with these items until pay-day on Saturday. And as the shopkeeper writes her account into the blue-backed exercise book that contains the full economic history of each villager, the woman admires the sweet, angelic faces of the chubby Dionne quintuplets in the Palmolive soap advertisement, painted in technicolor on the piece of metal nailed on to the door of the shop.

Since this is a workday, she will not have the time or energy, after a harrowing day in the fields, to cook the type of meal she would prepare on a Sunday.

Smoked Ham Hocks with Lima Beans, Pig Tails and Rice is a meal that don't take much time or cost much to prepare. If you is a working woman or a working man, and you come home from work hot and sweaty and tired, and you don't have much time to prepare a meal, particular if you have children to feed, why don't you try your hand at cooking this meal too?

You need a pint o' lima beans. In these modern days, you could buy lima beans in plastic bags, by the pound, in any supermarket. First thing you do when you get home is to wash off and soak the lima beans in warmish water, picking out the beans that spoil.

Leave the beans to soak for a while. Or, you could have soak' them overnight. And likewise with the pig tails. Soak them overnight to get out the salt, nuh. That way, you could avoid having to boil and boil the pig tails, and having to throw off the water and fill-back-up the saucepan with cold water the next day.

Wash off two or three whole pig tails. A whole pig tail is one cut from the poor pig's "botsy" right down to end of the tail. Dry them off on a towel. And with a sharp knife, cut the pig tails at the joints to make them more manageable when you put them in a saucepan or a pot.

Cut up some fresh green onions (we call them eschalots back in the Wessindies, but up here in Canada a "'shalot" is not the same thing as a green onion!) and about three medium-sized cloves o' garlic, and put them, along with the pig tails, in a hotted-up frying pan, preferable one made out o' iron, with some oil in it.

Add in a little black pepper and some fresh thyme (if you don't have fresh thyme, dry thyme will do). And brown the pig tails, turning them over constantly so they don't stick to the bottom o' the frying pan and burn. You are not intending to cook the pig tails in this oil, you're just searing them.

When the pig tails are brown, take them out of the frying pan and put them in a saucepan with water. Remember: throw away the oil and the garlic and the thyme that you put in the frying pan to sear the pig tails with. These things are not good for your system. They have in too much salt and too much grease for North Amurcans. Most Wessindians just *love* this grease. But you don't have to pretend you is a Wessindian and eat all this grease. Although, once in a blue moon, a little grease or fat never kill nobody!

Bring the pig tails to a rapid boil, then turn down the heat to medium-low. If the heat is too high, the pig tails, which have in certain things, going foam and boil over and mess up your stove, and you going have to spend time cleaning it off. So, caution yourself. With a medium-low heat, your pig tails going start to cook nice and slow. They going still give off that white, thickish, foamy scum on top the water. All you got to do is ladle it off.

Even at this stage, after the saucepan boil the first time, you still have time to taste the water, to test if too much saltiness left back in the pig tails. And if this is the case, pour off the whole saucepan of water and full it back up with cold water. And bring it to a next boil.

Never cook pig tails in such a way that, when you serve them, the meat is stringy. All that stringiness in the meat will get between your teeth and your dentures when you bite down on a nice-looking piece. It will only cause you to have to go to the dentist. A pig tail that is well cooked should be soft — but not too soft. If you cook them too soft, oh loss!, the skin going burst and drop off the bone.

If you are spending all this time so far, preparing this simple meal, you might feel a little peckish for a drink. And it is natural. So, pour yourself something. A Banks beer from Barbados. Banks is the best beer in the world. A Jamaican would tell you that Red Stripe is the best. A Trinidadian would say that Carib is the best. But don't mind them Jamaicans and Trinidadians. Stick to the best: Banks beer from Barbados.

When the pig tails have reached a certain softness, add in the lima beans in the same pot and let them cook at a medium or low heat. Keep your two eyes on them beans, hear. Keep a eagle eye on them beans. And pour off the white foam that form at the top, or skim it off with a spoon. Whilst watching the beans like a hawk, you could be washing out the frying pan that you seared the pig tails in.

Historically, this food was cooked in one pot. Back in the slave days, the woman cooking this food probably had only one utensil to her name in which to cook her food. But cooking any kind of peas or beans in the same pot as you cook rice is a very tricky thing to do. Sometimes, the peas or the beans does be cooked, and when you hear the shout, the damn rice grains does be hard. At other times, the rice does be cooked soft, and oh Lord, the peas or the beans does be hard as bullets.

Each of the three ingreasements in this meal — the rice, the lima beans and the pig tails — have to be cook to the same softness. If you are not an expert at cooking peas and rice in the same pot, at the same time, you should cook them in two separate pots, at the same time.

But you won't, in spite of a modern sophistication, want to put a blemish upon that culinary tradition of the geography of food, would you? No! After all, the purpose of cooking rice and beans with pig tails is to give taste and sweetness to the rice and beans. My mother, like most Wessindian women, always say that you have to season the water you cook rice in with a piece o' salt meat. "To put little goodness in the water, boy!"

When I was growing up, the salt meat my mother used to boil in the water for the rice, or in the water for soup, was the sweetest thing in the world. And sometimes, my mother would take out a piece o' salt meat from the boiling pot and put it in my mouth, to "keep the wolves from the door," and to keep me quiet. Sometimes, too, it was not always completely cooked; this is why I know so much about stringy pig tails. And always, the little gift of meat from my mother's pot was mouth-burningly hot. But it was an act of love, just as when a mother in North America, making a cake, gives her child a lick of the spoon that mixes the batter, or of the bowl when she is finished with it.

When I got bigger and could withstand the hotness of boiling water, I would myself try to extricate from my mother's pot a little piece of the pig tail or salt beef. And always I would suffer the same burning of the mouth, the same searing discomfort, the penalty for the transgression of trespassing upon the domain of her cooking.

Once, I saw a piece bubbling amongst the dry peas. It was a small piece. Just the top was visible in the raging bubbles of the "broiling" water of the soup. My hand was ready to pounce upon it when I heard her steps coming from the shed-roof into the kitchen. I had to hide the evidence in my closed mouth. The pain sent shivers up my palate. And as I remained silent in my agony, my mother chose that moment to engage me in conversation.

"You was practising today for the 880 after school? That you get in this house so late? You think you going win the 880 on Sports Day?"

I could not speak. She looked at me in some surprise, and she herself stopped speaking. She stood in shock at my disrespect in not answering her. But I could not. I could not move. Then, all of a sudden, I no longer felt any pain. The pain became like a chloroform to my senses. I had swallowed the joint of pig tail, *whole*.

It was the last time I tried to steal pig tail from any pot she was cooking. And to this day, I never taste the pot of anything at all that I myself am cooking.

"Once burnt, twice shy!"

Cooking food is an adventure, and you have to take risks. You can't expect your food to come out perfect each time you try your hand at something, as if you're cooking from a blueprint. Trial and error is the motto.

Remember the women in the olden days, who had to use sticks and dried pieces o' sugar cane, or dried mahogany pods, for fuel? And how they had to pull out a piece o' wood from under the pot to regulate the heat? And then place it back to increase the heat? All the time getting their two hands scorch and burn up?

Trial and error. There wasn't no button marked "high" or "medium" or "simmer" in them days, to regulate the heat under a pot o' food. So if you are brave, and think you still want to handle this Wessindian meal, let's get back to the lima beans.

They're going to take a little more longer to cook than the rice. Particular, if you didn't soak the beans in water overnight. Use a spoon to take out one, and press it between your thumb and index finger to see how they're coming. When they have reached the stage just before they are soft, it's time to put the rice in the same pot. Bring the pot to a boil and turn the heat down immediately to simmer, with the lid tightly on.

"The worst have passed," as my mother used to say.

Start preparing the smoked ham hocks. There is nothing appealing in the shape or form or size of a smoked ham hock. You see skin. You see fat. You see bone. And sometimes, if the butcher isn't careful, you does see bristles of the pig's hair running all over the ham hock! You may have to extract these hairs with a tweezers, or cut out parts o' the skin that hold the hair with a sharp knife. An uncooked ham hock may not be pleasant to behold; but when it is cooked, it's the epitome of culinary beauty, the essence of Barbadian hot-cuisine.

Wash off the smoked ham hocks and dry them with a kitchen towel. Boil them till you can feel that the skin soft. Cut each hock in half, following the bone, from one end to the other. Take out the bone, and cut those halves into half again, making quarters. Some people cook the ham hock whole and then cut it up after it's cooked. I prefer to serve ham hocks without the bone; you have enough bones in the pig tails already.

A woman who knows her oats, cooking-wise, and who could handle herself in the kitchen, would put both the smoked ham hocks and the lima beans to cook in the same pot with the pig tails. But don't try that: you would be asking for bare trouble. Because you aren't no expert, yet!

Get a large saucepan or a large frying pan. Put some oil in the pan with lots of sliced onions, two heads of green onions, two cloves of garlic sliced or pressed, fresh thyme if you have it (otherwise dried thyme), pepper (black pepper seeds or as many fresh hot peppers as you can stomach) and one tablespoon of coconut cream. Mix in these ingreasements and bring them to a hotness. When they are sawtayed, put the sliced ham hocks into this sizzling goodness, and turn down the heat.

Stir now and then. A good way of knowing when to stir is, every other time you take a sip of your beer, stir slowly and gently. It does do something to your head and to your pot. Cover the pan to keep in the in-goodness.

After fifteen minutes, slice up a big, fresh red tomato and let the slices sit on top of the ham hocks. If you reach this stage without getting drunk or burning up the food, yuh going good-good-good! Cover-back-down the pan. Ham hocks must not be too gristly; they should be soft and succulent.

Back in the slave days there wasn't no serving dishes and no great number of plates. People didn't get no sets of plates and dishes as wedding gifts! So, you would get your food piled high-high-high, on an enamel plate. Like a small Everest. But we don't have to retread those paths to the slave days in order to reproduce and enjoy the culinary preciousness of slave food!

To serve, place one large pot-spoon o' rice on each plate. Beside the rice, which you have stirred so that the lima beans are equally distributed in it, place one nice, juicy piece o' pig tail with the rice grains scraped off. And beside the pig tail, place a generous serving o' ham hocks.

Salad and dessert are not intended to go with this food. To serve a salad would digress too radically from the cultural origin of this food and destroy its authenticity. This is not the time for graciousness and sophistication, as if you're dreaming of hot-cuisines from France and Italy! You are not inviting the Prime Minister's wife, or the Lieutenant-Governor. So don't serve no salad. And no dessert, at all, at all. To Wessindians, dessert is something you need to add to a meal if the food is too light in the first place and you need to full-up everybody's belly. Dessert is just a way of propping up food. And this food is already heavy. It was intended for men and women who used to toil in the sugar-cane fields sixteen hours a day, and was meant to keep their bellies full, for the whole day and night.

My mother used to say that it is the "glue" in the ham hocks, mixed with the freshness in the lima beans, plus all the other ingreasements, that does make this food "cloyed" you, meaning that it going stick to your ribs and make you feel that you could move the earth. Or make love or dipsy-doodle all night, and next morning too.

Your presentation of this food could also include the music you play whilst eating. The slaves used to have fife and drum, and a hair comb with paper over the teeth: an improvised mouth-organ or harmonica. I suggest a rousing calypso. But not one by Harry Belafonte; he isn't a real calypso singer! Choose the real McCoy: *any* calypso by the Trinidadian singer Crazy. Or by the Mighty Sparrow. If your religion forbids this kind o' music, turn on the radio to a church service and hope you hear "The Day Thou Gavest, Lord, is Ended." You will see the irony. This hymn is perhaps the best alternative.

There is a little something you learn when you eat this kind o' food. Lima beans does taste more better when served with pork. There is something in the lima beans that, when put next to a piece o' pork, does bring out a tantalizing taste that defies description. The way you assemble a spoonful of the ingreasements is as important as the food itself. In the same spoon, or on the same fork, you should have a little rice, a piece o' pig tail, a slice o' ham hock and lima beans, to taste in one mouthful. You never, with this kind of food, take a mouthful of rice by itself and eat it. Or a mouthful of lima beans and eat it. Or pig tail only. Or ham hock only. The delicious combination of these four ingreasements is like seeing the end of a journey.

"Boy, lima beans and plain rice, with smoked ham hocks?" my mother would say, smacking her lips, with a fine line of oil running down her chin. "*This* is food! This is *hot-cuisine*, boy!"

The saltiness in the pig tails, and the starch in the lima beans, and the "glue" in the smoked ham hocks will cause you to drink a lot of water, or other liquids. The preferred beverage for this food was swank, which is available in the cane fields and rum shops of Barbados. But here in North Amurca, "yuh can't put your hand on it," it ain't available. But as my mother always say, "If you don't have a horse, ride a cow. Or a jackass. Or a mule." That is the philosophy of cultural improvisation.

So, find a Wessindian store and buy something called mauby bark. Soak a few pieces o' bark in water for a few hours; strain it through a strainer; add a few ice-cubes; drop in a few drops o' white rum; sugar to taste, and *bram!* you have a suitable alternative. Mauby.

Suppose the people in your house, this blessed evening, don't eat off all the food? Lord have his mercy! Don't worry. In the morning, this food going taste more better when you warm it up.

Smoked Ham Hocks with Lima Beans

When we left back food in Barbados, when I was a boy, we kept it in the oven, with the heat turned off of course, to prevent ants, usually red ants, from devouring the food. Red ants can easily camouflage themselves amongst the colours of food, and are hardly visible. They could eat their bellyful of a plate of steamed red snapper served with tomatoes boiled-down in rice, and never be detected!

We also kept food in the larder. But the larder had to be protected from the attacks of these red ants. We did this by placing each of the larder's legs in a tin filled with kerosene oil mixed with water.

It was always our belief that food left over tastes sweeter the next day, because all the ingreasements have had time to work themselves in with one another. When you warm up the Smoked Ham Hocks with Lima Beans, Pig Tails and Rice for the next eating, good-Jesus-Christ-have-his-mercy! Talk about food tasting sweet?

Note: Whilst I was writing out this way of cooking Smoked Ham Hocks with Lima Beans, Pig Tails and Rice, I myself was listening to the Trinidadian calypsonian Crazy singing "Paul, Yuh Mother Comes" and win'ing my waist and "doing bad" — all by myself! So, what happen to you that you can't shake up your body line too? Move, man! Show me your motions, girl!

King-Fish and White Rice

The seas round Barbados used to be inhabited by one of the sweetest fish in the world: the flying fish. But Barbadians cooked the fish that used to live in the sea surrounding the island so damn bad, drowning them with too much lime juice, seasoning and pepper sauce, and then frying them too long in oil, that all the fish — especially the flying fish — got vex and swim away from Barbados. Nowadays, most of the fish that was native to Barbados can be found in Trinidad waters.

Barbadian housewives and children, and all the foreign cooks in hotels, blame the Barbadian fishermen for this loss.

And the women that does sell fry fish. They don't shed a tear when a Barbadian fisherman drown, or get lost on the high seas, trying to sneak into Trinidadian waters to steal back, or hijack, a few flying fish.

It is a crying shame that the fish have emigraded from Barbadian waters. But it serve the Barbadians right. They really used to kill the natural taste of the fish by using tum-much seasoning, and frying the fish deep deep in a lot o' lard oil. They cooked all the in-goodness out. The fish was burn up and dry. And you use to feel as if you was eating fried balata rubber!

There are places in Barbados, like Baxters Road, Oistins and Sin-Lawrence Gap, where any night of the week you can see droves o' tourisses eating fry fish, with all the lard oil running down both sides o' their mouths — and enjoy-ing it. "This is the best fish I ever taste!" the tourisses say, as they devour the fish. But tourisses are not arbiters of good fry fish.

Why do Barbadians wash fish or soak it in lime juice till they wash off all the fish taste? Because they hate the smell of fish. So, by the time they're done with it, you don't know if you eating fish or if you eating pork; they taste the same way.

The poor fish had no other alternative but to run to Trinidad, as refugees, to save their cultural identity.

If you want a flying fish in Barbados nowadays, you have to import one. As a matter of fact, flying fish are eas-ier to get in Toronto than in Barbados. If you are living in

North Amurca and your mouth should water for some flying fish, you can't buy just one to eat, you have to buy a half-dozen — and frozen to boot. And when you look at the package, it says, "Manufractured in Trinidad"! What the hell do Trinidadians know about flying fish?

The only fish of quality that you can get in Barbados nowadays is king-fish or dolphin. Sometimes a cavalley, or ning-nings, or barbaras, or sprats. Sharks are plentiful, including those of a political nature. The Ministry of Fisheries still don't know why sharks are so plentiful in Barbadian waters. It took an expert from Canada to tell Barbadians the reason: sharks were sent from Trinidad to look for Barbadian fishermen to feed off.

King-fish has a silvery appearance and looks just like a bigger version of a flying fish — a cousin almost. So Barbadians have come to love their king-fish. King-fish is a strong fish, meaning it has a strong taste. The meat is not delicate like a trout; it is white and sweeter.

King-fish can be served at a formal occasion or at a private dinner, if you want to impress your girlfriend or boyfriend. But don't try cooking the whole king-fish. If you buy a whole king-fish, you'll have to scale it and clean out all the guts. Most people either don't know how or don't like to scale fish. And many do not like to see a fish head, with its two eyes, like balls of lead, staring at them from a dinner plate.

"I can't bear to see the head! Take it away!" a Canadian woman told me and a baked king-fish, one night at dinner. "Take it off before you bring it to the table. Those eyes are staring at me like . . . like . . ."

If you have a weak stomach when it comes to seeing the insides of a fish, I suggest you buy king-fish steaks. The man at the fish store would have scaled the fish and taken out most of the guts already — all those things Jonah could tell you are to be found in the belly of a fish.

When you bring the king-fish steaks home, soak them in water that have in lemon juice, from a piece o' lemon. Then, with the same piece o' lemon, rub it all over the fish — all over, particularly around the bones in the spine. Rinse off the steaks and dry them, or leave them to dry 'pon a piece o' paper towel.

King-fish steaks that are boiled don't taste too good. You have to fry these steaks, even if it is against your principles concerning fats and cholesterols. You won't be feasting on fried king-fish steaks *every* night, after all!

You're going fry the fish in a nice batter made with a mixture o' flour and breadcrumbs; fifty-fifty is a good proportion, but use any combination that you prefer. Add salt and white pepper to the flour and breadcrumbs, and mix it up. The reason for using white pepper and not black is that the king-fish already have a heavy flavour, and you want to use a lighter pepper to balance off that heaviness.

But suppose you don't have white pepper? Use black pepper and take the consequences.

Now it's time to beat the eggs (the number depends on the amount of fish you're cooking) till all you can see is yellow. Beat them and beat them, and beat them with a fork.

Put some olive oil, or butter, or ordinary lard oil in your frying pan and warm it up. When the oil in the frying pan is hot enough that, when you drop the first steak in it, you going hear the frying pan whisper *Zzzzz*, that mean she ready to take the steaks.

Dip each one of the king-fish steaks in the egg and, fast-fast, put it in the batter of flour mixed with bread-crumbs, coating both sides. One by one, put the steaks in the frying pan. You going hear a nice sweet *Zzzzz!*-sound each time a steak touch the frying pan and the hot oil start to seal the fish. And the first thing you got to do when the steaks are in the pan is to put a knife, or a fork, or a spatula under each one, to make sure that she not sticking to the pan and burning up before she done cook. When one side get brown, turn it over and let the other side get golden brown too. Then take them out.

Unless you are the kind o' person who don't like fats, you could use the same oil you fry the steaks in to make the gravy. Cut up some green onions — not regular onions, since the king-fish have such a strong flavour — and some fresh thyme, and add them to the frying pan with enough salt and pepper to suit your taste. Cook the green onions a little and then add in some white wine — or any other kind o' spirits or liquor that you happen to have — and cook it over a low heat. Just for spite, add in a lil more wine and a few drops o' Worcestershire sauce.

If this sauce turning out too whitey-whitey and you want it to be more brown, add a drop o' colouring. I won't advise you to use no Chinese colouring, because that have-in too much salt. I does make my own colouring. Do you know how to make colouring? It easy.

Get a small saucepan and pour some brown sugar in it. If you don't have no Demerara brown sugar, you could use sugar that white. Over a medium heat, stir and stir the sugar until it melt and start to resemble syrup or molasses. Continue stirring until it turn black and thick and all the sugar dissolve into liquid that is black. Now you have a good Barbadian colouring.

Put a touch o' this colouring in the sauce and you going see how the sauce turn brown — or even black if you not careful. And after you use the amount that you need, put the rest in the fridge for future use.

In the olden days in Barbados, when we wanted to make colouring, we'd get a empty tot that had in Canadian salmon or Carnation Milk or imported canned peas. Into this can we would pour some sugar and stir and stir and stir until our two hands get tired. But we still continued stirring, until the consistency of the sugar change and turn syrupy, and then black like tar. Back then, we never throw-away the tin that we make colouring in. We used to keep the tin and christen it "the colouring tot." A family would use the same colouring tot for thirty, forty years, till all o' them dead off, before they would throw-it-way their colouring tot and get a new one.

In North Amurca, you don't have to worry your head over making colouring or preserving a colouring tot. Neither in Canada nor in Amurca do cooks really know anything about a colouring tot as a heirloom. To-besides, you can buy a bottle o' colouring in any supermarket.

So, now that the king-fish steaks and gravy are ready, what you going to eat with them? You should have decided this beforehand. But since you didn't, here is a little advice.

The thing about eating food that cook sweet is to make sure it has a good combination o' tastes and colours. You have to know the taste of king-fish, of plain white rice and of Wessindian sweet potatoes or yams. And when you understand the significance of these different tastes, you have to know what other tastes to put with them. So, in addition to cooking some plain rice (peas and rice is too strong to use with king-fish), how about cooking some sweet potatoes or yams? And to bring out the full flavour of the king-fish, how about making some cucumber prickle?

Slice some cucumber thin-thin, and put them in a bowl. Add a dash of salt; a few pieces of fresh hot pepper cut up small-small-small; a generous amount of freshly squeezed lemon juice; and a lot o' fresh parsley leaves pick-off and drop in the bowl. Stir all this round and leave it to sit.

And then you going see the combination o' colours: the golden brown of the king-fish steak; the whiteness o' the white rice; sweet potatoes the colour o' gold; and the light green of the cucumber prickle! And won't all these colours look good on a white china plate, with a blue or gold border, the colours of crockery that royalty does use?

When you serve the king-fish steaks, add a lil gravy on top o' each one — or on the rice or the sweet potato.

These king-fish steaks is the best substitute for the emigrating flying fish. But suppose you did-have some frozen flying fish? You could cook them the same way. But you shouldn't leave them frying in the frying pan as long as the king-fish, 'cause they would get hard and dry the way they does-do fry fish up in Sin Lawrence Gap where the tourisses does congregate to eat.

The important thing about fish is that when it cook, it should still be soft and succulent. And it *must* smell and taste a lil fishy, to remind you that, after all, you are eating fish.

Meal-Corn Cou-Cou

very Wessindian island would claim that they invent cou-cou. Don't believe them. Cou-cou, along with other elements of superior cultural and gastronomical significance, a significance that stretch to every land in the world — as little as this significance might seem to the bigness of a North Amurcan consciousness and sensibility — have all been born, invented, started first or originated in that small paradise of an island, Barbados.

We could probably trace the origin of cou-cou back to *foo-foo* or some such African dish; or to *funji*, as it is called in Sin-Kitts; or to *polenta*, which is what Italians does-call a dish that look like cou-cou but which isn't. So, if we was disposed to attribute to this simple but pleasurable dish a larger African or European significance, we could call it by one o' them fancy-fancy foreign names. But the incontrovertible truth is that cou-cou, a dish made from corn that you grind-up, fine-fine-fine, into a meal and cook in water that have okras boil in it, was first cooked in Barbados. From there, it spread all over the world.

It is a historical fact that in Barbados, the slaves was the first people to cook and eat cou-cou. Imagine a few slaves, working their fingers to the bone under the hot sun on a plantation.

"This sun hot as shite!" they say to one another. "Hot hot hot!"

Sweat pouring off their back, and the Plantation manager, his head covered with a cork hat or a sun helmet, cock-off on his horse like a living statue of a conquering general, holding a whip in his hand like Lord Wellington or Thomas Jefferson. The bastard (in truth and in fact, since he was usually the "outside child" of the Plantation owner) would drive the slaves and drive them; and drive some lashes with his whip made out o' cow-skin, or balata, or a limb from a tamarind tree, "Wap! Wap! Wap!" in their arse. All day.

When the Plantation bell ring to announce that work done, it is six o'clock. The slaves had worked from dawn till sunset. And when they start to crawl home to their shacks, tired tired tired and hungry hungry hungry, and dying for something to eat to full-up their belly quick with, so they could last through the night and face the next day, it was cou-cou they revert to — cou-cou, the cheapest, fastest food in them slave-wukking circumstances to cook.

Any enterprising slave woman would have a few okra trees growing behind her shack. And she plant them outta the eyes of the manager, and outta the sight of her envious, malicious neighbours. Some o' her neighbours was like crabs, always pulling her down.

To plant a okra tree, all you have to have is a dried okra. The seeds from the okra does fall out easy, and all you got to do is drop a few seeds in the ground. Before the bell in the Plantation yard ring the next morning, *bram!* a okra tree growing in your backyard. Or almost as fast as that.

The Plantation didn't spend tummuch time finding nice food for the slaves to eat. Some slaves uses to get a lil allowance of food, from the food that the Plantation uses to throw away. Cheap food. Ends o' food. The "leavings" o' food. Skin and bones and fat and grizzle. Some o' it was corn. The slaves plant this corn and watch it grow in splendour in the Plantation field, plentiful as heavenly bounty, greener than the waves of the sea round Barbados, more greener and pretty than the waves o' the Atlantic Ocean that bring them here to Barbados. And they see this green beauty almost all year round. And almost all year round they couldn't touch one. They had to thief some.

If a slave didn't eat all her corn when it was "green," meaning fresh, then she would have some left back to dry in the sun on the roof of her shack. She would husk the dried corn and pound it with a rock-stone till it got fine fine and turn to meal. Eventually the slaves invented a thing to grind the corn in, to make a more finer corn meal. And with this meal they start to make cou-cou.

Since then, cou-cou have taken on a serious cultural and sociological significance in Barbados. When you want to be sure that the woman you intend to marry is the right woman, the first question you does put to her mother is, "Can your daughter turn meal-corn? Can she turn a mellow cou-cou?"

If the answer to this simple, but loaded, question is in the negative, *bram!* straightaway you run out of your former mother-in-law-to-be's drawing room, and you start looking for another potential mother-in-law. And when you find her, you ask the same question, "Can your daughter turn a cou-cou?"

"Child," your prospective mother-in-law will say to you, "I like you as a son-in-law. For my daughter — yes! How you mean? My daughter can't only turn cou-cou sweet sweet sweet, she does turn it mellow mellow too! Like anything! Yes. How you mean? Why you don't let me call her now, to turn some meal-corn cou-cou for you?"

This is the answer you been looking for! This is the woman you been looking for. Married-she-off, right now.

But if you isn't a Barbadian, I have to caution you about putting this question to her, for to ask whether a woman can turn cou-cou sweet sweet does not refer only to turning cou-cou! In the local vernacular it can also mean something else, something more serious. So, when you ask this question, you could also be asking, through implication, whether the girl in question "have a certain proclivity" — whether the girl is good in bed. And you don't want your prospective mother-in-law to think that *that* is all you have on your mind concerning her nice, Christian-minded, well-brought-up daughter. She might run you outta her drawing room with a frying pan to your head, or with her cou-cou stick in your arse!

So, you have to clothe your question in the proper diplomatic language and with the correct tone o' voice. Actually, the best thing to do is not to ask the girl's mother. Instead, ask the girl's friend to ask her cousin to ask the mother, "Can so-and-so, you know who, turn cou-cou?"

If you find a woman who can turn cou-cou mellow and slow and sweet-sweet, then you have found gold. And everlasting happiness. The right woman, simple as that.

What is the reason for this heavy reliance on a woman's skill and facility with cou-cou? Simple: cou-cou that is not stirred good, and slow slow, and mellow, ends up with lumps in it. And lumps in cou-cou are portentous and symbolic of the lumps your marriage to the wrong woman will be infested with; of the hardships that lie in wait for you; of the heartache that will face you in accumulated bitterness, at the end of each week, every Saturday, when cou-cou is eaten in every household throughout the land.

To make a sweet cou-cou, you'll need a cou-cou stick. In fact, you should know all there is to know about this very important Barbadian implement. Every self-respecting Barbadian home has a cou-cou stick. It has a piece o' twine attached to it with which to hang it from a nail in the kitchen. Not to have a cou-cou stick in your home is like a North Amurcan home without a measuring cup, or an Italian home without a *pentola per gli spaghetti*. Actually, I can't think of anything so essential to a North Amurcan household as a cou-cou stick is to Barbadian culture. A cou-cou stick makes a home a Barbadian home.

It is about twelve to fourteen inches long, made outta durable wood, like wallaba, and shaped like a paddle with a narrower handle. After it is used and washed, it is greased or rubbed down with butter, lard or oil, to keep it moist and prevent it from splintering. In one household, in one life-time, there is no need for a second cou-cou stick. A cou-cou stick is more durable than love.

But the cou-cou stick has a usage other than its primary, culinary one; it is also used as a weapon. Women use it to beat cheating, lying, worthless, two-timing men. And recalcitrant children know the sting of a cou-cou stick. In general, throughout the culture, it is the metaphor used to raise and instil fear. Just raise a cou-cou stick in your hand, and order and silence reign.

I remember the times the cou-cou stick was pulled, in rage, from its pride of place, and was placed instead, with stinging, multiplying effect, on my backside.

"Boy, you won't hear!" my mother say, delivering her blows in the same rhythm as her words. "You won't hear!"

The cou-cou stick. A blessed instrument. An instrument of durability. An instrument of discipline. An instrument essential for the preparation of hot-cuisine.

Of course, in places like Toronto or Brooklyn, where there is a different civilization — or "no civilization at all," as my mother says — and usually no cou-cou sticks (unless you're in a Barbadian home), a large wooden spoon can be used as a substitute. But if you want a mellow cou-cou, you need a real cou-cou stick. All you have to do to get one is walk into any Wessindian store that sells salt fish and sweet potatoes and pig tails, and ask the woman behind the counter, "You got a cou-cou stick, that I could buy off you?"

If you don't look Wessindian, she going roll her two eyes and quizz-up her face, asking herself, "Wha' she know 'bout cou-cou stick?" Yes! If you don't look a lil like a Wessindian, she going open her two eyes big big in wonder, and look at you funny. She may even say to herself, "What the arse I hearing? Hows he know 'bout a cou-cou stick?" But she going still sell you one.

Now that you got your cou-cou stick, you ready to make some rich, mellow cou-cou. Here are the steps.

Number one: Slice up a few okras. Up here in North Amurca, you does have real nice okras. And these okras does be packaged and frozen. Personally, I prefer the frozen okras to the fresh ones. To cook with them, you don't even have to thaw them. All you got to do is slice them up whilst they still frozen and drop them in a pot with a pinch o' salt. Bring them to a boil. When the okra-water look yellow and thick, take them off the fire.

Number two: Pour off most of the water and okras into a large Pyrex bowl. Leff-back some water in the pot you going cook the cou-cou in. Turn down the heat now to low.

Number three: Ladle-off the okras and dump them in the pot that is on the low heat.

Number four: Now you need some corn meal. There is two kind o' meal-corn you could use: one is a little coarse, while the other is fine. If you want a "balanced" cou-cou that won't be too pappy or too stiff, mix the coarse corn meal and the fine corn meal half-and-half. You can't go wrong! Pour in lil of the corn meal mixture into the pot — about one-half the amount you want to cook — and start stirring, using wrist-work.

Stirring cou-cou is a art. You have to stir from the bottom, and in the same motion stir round the side of the pot, using your wrist in the action more than your whole arm. And after each action o' stirring, you got to wipe off the excess corn meal from the cou-cou stick and from the side of the pot, and mix she in with the rest of the corn meal, and continue stirring, and stirring, and stirring . . .

When you try to find out if a woman can turn cou-cou good good (apart from its obvious sexual connotation), you're really trying to find out if, when she stirring slow-slow, she still leaving back little balls o' uncooked corn meal mingled with the rest of the cou-cou. To prevent this from happening to you — if you are not a master of cooking cou-cou — all you have to do is put half the corn meal you intend to cook in a bowl and pour cold water over it. Leave it until the water absorb all the corn meal.

Some people does pour all the meal in a bowl and cover it with the water — but this is cheating. When you's a master at cou-cou, you don't need to soak none of the meal-corn in no water at all.

But suit yourself. The important thing is that you don't want lumps in your cou-cou. Lumps are a cultural embarrassment with serious sexual connotations, especially for a Barbadian woman cooking cou-cou.

You need to be able to control the body, or the stiffness of the cou-cou. The best way of doing this is to add a lil corn meal if the consistency of the cou-cou is too much like pap; or add a lil okra-water if the cou-cou is too stiff. If all the okra-water is put in at the same time, you can't easily control the stiffness of your cou-cou.

So keep the heat under the cou-cou still turned to low, hear? When she stirring good, you going notice that it still need some more okra-water. So, pour in a lil more. And keep stirring she.

Number five: Add in some more meal, and add in some more okra-water. Keep stirring she.

Number six: Stop stirring, and cover down the pot. Let she simmer. And steam. You going know when she simmer long enough, because you going see lil bubbles jumping up and down inside the pot.

Number seven: If the meal still thick in the pot, and if you want your cou-cou to come out a lil more thinner, add in a lil more okra-water and stir she some more. By this time your cou-cou *must* be done cooking. You have stirred she for twenty, twenty-five minutes. You gotta take patience with stirring a good cou-cou, like in other things.

Number eight: Cover-back-down the pot, and let the cou-cou coagulate inside the pot.

Number nine: This is cou-cou. It done.

Now, for the serving of the cou-cou to your guesses. You should have at least one measuring cup o' okra-water leff-back in the Pyrex bowl. This is where it coming in useful.

Get a fresh bowl, about six inches in diameter and four inches deep. Ladle-out a tablespoonful o' okra-water (or a lil butter) and pour it in the bowl. Ladle-out a big pot spoon o' cou-cou from the pot and put it in the small bowl. Shake the bowl in a circular motion, turning she round and round, and you going find that the cou-cou form itself into a nice smooth ball; hence the term, "ball o' cou-cou." Dip the tablespoon back in the okra-water and pass it all over the ball o' cou-cou, till it come like a lil yellow bowling ball, or a small grapefruit, round round. This is cou-cou, man!

Since you are no longer a slave, you not eating the cou-cou plain. Cou-cou is a traditional dish and you must serve it with traditional things. Like boil' sweet potatoes — not yams, but Wessindian sweet potatoes. And a cucumber prickle which you know how to make already. You don't *dare* say you serving cou-cou without intending to have sweet potatoes and cucumber prickle and avocado pear with it!

And you'll need something more. Cou-cou is culturally associated with flying fish. But if you do not remember your cultural roots (and since the flying fish fled to Trinidad), you can serve cou-cou with can-salmon, salt fish or a nice Bajan stew, all of which are more readily available in North Amurca than seasonal, slippery flying fish.

Bajan (the endearing term for Barbadian) stew has pieces o' pork and pieces o' beef, and lots o' tomatoes and onions in she, and the sauce does be dark and *sweet*. And when I tell you sweet? Sweet for so!

If you choose to have can-salmon, try making a butter sauce to go with it. It easy easy. Put a frying pan on the stove and add in some butter (or the oil), some fresh thyme, some salt — but not too much, since the can-salmon have in salt — and some fresh hot pepper or black pepper, and bring these to a nice heat. Then turn down the heat.

Whilst they simmering inside the pan, add in a tin o' can-salmon (or even two tins!), including the water that comes in the can with the salmon, and stir slow and gentle. Add-in some more cold water and cook until the sauce is heated through.

The most important thing 'bout the serving of food down there in Barbados and the Wessindies is the quantity. Down there, in all that hot sun, people does eat a lot o' food. You ever see a Wessindian man siddown behind a ball o' cou-cou? The plate does be pile high, so damn high that you could barely see his face even if he sitting opposite you!

And the cou-cou does be served hot. Hot hot hot. It is generally not normal to serve or eat food unless it is piping hot. When we serve cold food to somebody, it is food cook a long time, hours before. This cold food, serve so, is regarded as an insult. And some women, who either like to eat cold food or does serve it cold, are sometimes nick-named "Cold food," pronounced as one word.

Perhaps eating hot food has something to do with the humidity in the island. Sometimes the humidity is unbearable. Eating food that is piping hot brings out a delicious sweat on your face and opens up all your pores. My mother tell me so. So, is so!

Some men, whilst they're eating cou-cou, *always* have a towel drape over one shoulder to mop away the sweat caused from eating hot food. But you don't have to carry on so! You don't need to be so culturally pure, and serve any linen napkins and bath towels to put round your guesses shoulders, when you serve them your nice ball o' cou-cou. You're not back in Barbados . . .

Get a plate that have enough deepness to hold gravy, and flip a small, dainty ball o' steaming-hot cou-cou plumb in the middle. 'Side o' the ball, place some Bajan stew or can-salmon or whatever flesh you serving the cou-cou with. Next to the stew or fish, place two slices o' sweet potato. And next to the potato, a tablespoonful o' cucumber prickle. If you have avocado, a slice o' that too! Take your tablespoon and make a dent in the middle of the ball o' cou-cou, like a crater. This lil crater is to hold the gravy that you intend to pour into it, until it run down the sides of the ball o' cou-cou, like hot lava does run down the side of a volcano.

When you eat this cou-cou, two things going happen to you. Number one, you going start sweating; and number two, when you eat it and it settle in your stomach, you will have a hard time staying awake. A sluggish feeling that the slaves use to call "nigritis" will set in, and you bound to close your two eyes and have a lil nod, or a siesta, or a short snooze. *Bram!* And before you hear the shout, you sound asleep. And neither the manager nor the Plantation bell can prise you from your slumber till the next morning, when the bell ring five times to summons you back to hard labour and travail, working in the sugar-cane fields. But the cou-cou is in your belly, already.

Breadfruit Cou-Cou with Braising Beef

Captain Bligh was one o' the people who sail from England to Africa, carrying nails and muskets and knives and silk top hats to trade with the Africans, for slaves. And he would take these slaves to the Wessindies, and exchange them for sugar and molasses and rum, and silver and gold — wherever he could find some, especially in South Amurca, in places like Brazil — and sail back to England with these riches, thereby completing the Triangular Trade.

But Cap'n Bligh, as his sailors used to call him, was also a man who love fruits and flowers. He was a kind o' amateur botanist. And whilst the slaves was being dragged on board the HMS *Bounty*, his ship, ole Cap'n Bligh uses to be sitting down in the shade, with a piece o' lead pencil in his hand, drawing pretty flowers of all the exotic plants surrounding him, that he find in Africa.

Cap'n Bligh was not the only English "sea dog" to love Africa bad bad. There was another sea captain who loved Africa and Africans bad bad bad, even more better than Cap'n Bligh. That was John Newton, the feller who write that sweet song "Amazing Grace," which all black people in Amurca love to sing. Cap'n John Newton write this song whilst he was lashing and transporting slaves from Africa. Boy! Cap'n Bligh and Cap'n Newton! Boy!

But getting back to ole Cap'n Bligh. Nobody nowadays don't remember too much about him, except that he is the man who introduce breadfruits into the Wessindies. Appears that the English slave-holders on the sugar-cane Plantations, and the cotton Plantations in the Wessindies, didn't have enough food that was cheap enough and filling enough to feed the slaves with; so they called on Cap'n Bligh, with his love and knowledge o' plants and flowers, to introduce a fruit or a vegetable, something that the slaves in the Wessindies could eat to make them more bigger for Cap'n Bligh and the English and the Amurcans and people like Thomas Jefferson. Being a lover of botany, Cap'n Bligh hit on the breadfruit. And this "discovery" make slave-owners in Amurca, in the Wessindies and up in England love Cap'n Bligh even more better. Boy! Talk 'bout love and marriage.

Breadfruit Cou-Cou with Braising Beef

There is a lil whisper that used to go 'bout the place in regards to the introduction o' breadfruits down there in the Wessindies. Something that does happen after you eat breadfruit: the fragrance, of expectoration. Of bodily gas. After you eat breadfruit, the gas is so distinctive, and is sensed so far and wide and long, that the slave-catcher and the Plantation manager uses to love it and love slaves who eat breadfruit. The slaves could no longer hide! Not after a nice, heavy meal o' breadfruit cou-cou. The gas they passed betrayed them. My own mother tell me this.

But apart from the slave-thing, Cap'n Bligh really did the Wessindies a favour. At least he start planting breadfruit trees in Barbados. And breadfruit cou-cou, or boil breadfruit, or steam breadfruit, or roast breadfruit, or pickle breadfruit, and any other way you could cook this plant, have come in good-good, many a day, to put food in the belly of a lot o' poor people. From a bad, disreputable journey, a segment of the Middle Passage, a good thing spring up: a green and large harvest of breadfruits.

I can't remember how long it does take to watch a breadfruit seed grow into a big big tree and bear breadfruits; but I know that a breadfruit, when ripe, is the size of a football. Everybody know this. The whole o' Barbados have a saying that if your head is big and round, then you have a "breadfruit head."

Anyhow, to make breadfruit cou-cou, first thing, get a fair-size breadfruit, with the stem still on it. The stem is a inch to a inch and a half long. No more longer than that. To know if the breadfruit that you buy (and you can usually get one from a Wessindian store) is a ripe one, inspect the skin good. It have to be green, turning almost yellow.

Wash off the breadfruit and take the "milk" off all the skin. The milk is the white juice you see on the skin. Cut she up in half, cut each half in half, and each o' them halves in half. This way, it is more manageable to peel off the skin.

How much breadfruit you use depends on the number o' mouths you intend to feed. Half o' breadfruit should more than satisfy four very hungry mouths, at least.

When you cut open the breadfruit, you going see the "belly" or the "heart." This is the softy-softy part, the spongy-spongy part, almost similar to the inside of a punkin or a squash — although a breadfruit don't have them kind o' seeds that you see in a punkin or a squash. So, don't look for no seeds.

Just cut out the belly and throw it away, leaving back the firm part. Peel off the skin and put the pieces o' breadfruit in a saucepan o' cold water. Before you cover-she-down, sprinkle little salt over she. Breadfruit don't take too long to cook, only as long as a English potato. Test it with a fork to make sure she cook soft.

If you're using half o' breadfruit, you'll need about four to six fair-sized English potatoes. After peeling them and washing them off, you could put them to cook in the same saucepan with the breadfruit. If the pieces o' breadfruit finish cooking before the potatoes, take them out and put them in a Pyrex bowl. Don't let the potatoes cook so long that they start to mash up and fall to pieces.

You may not be the kind o' person who usually keeps pig tails or salt pork or salt beef in your fridge; but you are going to need some salt meat to give a little life to the breadfruit cou-cou. Any salt meat would do, but pig tails is preferable.

Remember to put the pig tails in water overnight — if you are a cook who likes to plan things — to soak-out the extra salt. Sear the pig tails by putting them in hot oil in a frying pan, with a little onion slice-up, two stems o' green onions slice-up and a garlic clove chop-up.

When the skin of the pig tails is seared, put them in a separate saucepan o' water to boil. You could boil them whole until they are soft, and then cut them at the joint; or you could cut them at the joint right away with a sharp kitchen knife, and then put them in the saucepan to boil. Just to remind you: don't use the left-over oil with the onions and things in it. Throw them out. Too much grease. Tummuch cholesterol.

Now you have two saucepans going. One have in the breadfruit and the English potatoes; the second one have in the pig tails boiling. Yuh going good now. So, why not fire one? Yuh can't be doing any kind o' serious cooking — except maybe boiling a egg — and tell me you're not firing a liquor! If you're cooking this meal on a Sunday, drink a rum and soda to cleanse your palate. But maintain concentration on what you cooking, though. If you are cooking this 'pon a Friday or a Saturday, take a beer. If religion or temperance forbid you to fire one, well, have a glass o' water, then — preferably warm, and with a pinch of salt in it. You would understand what I mean. But drink something; yuh going need it.

Time to prepare the real thing, the main part of the meal, namely, the braising beef. When I was a boy in Sin-Matthias village, the beef we uses to eat, like almost everything else, came from Away, from the Argentine.

"The Argenteen produces the best beef in the whirl!" my mother says. "More better than that thing the English send down here, called bully beef."

Beef was not our favourite. It was out of our reach, and was not a "stable" in our diet. The Joneses on Flagstaff Road (where I lived) and the Whittakers out the "front road" were the only two families who kept cows. Cows and flies. Flies in their thousands buzzing round the cow pens.

Early in the morning, at five o'clock, you would see Mr. Jones or Mr. Whittaker or some of their children taking their stocks — their cows — for a walk. The Joneses and Whittakers were big families with lots of boy-children and even more girl-children. It seem that the more cows you owned, the more children you had. The Joneses and the Whittakers had the largest families.

"Is the milk they does drink," my mother said. "And they don't have to buy it, neither!"

And sometimes, on those few occasions when I was permitted to "go to the sea," accompanied by an adult for safety, on a Sunday morning early early, I would see Mr. Whittaker or Mr. Jones or their children, taking their cows for a dip. Once, Mr. Whittaker took a horse. The horse pooped in the sea and we fled.

Cows were kept for milk, which we drank fresh every morning, filled with bubbles and a smell of the cow. There was no knowledge of the word "pasteurization." Sometimes Mr. Jones and Mr. Whittaker would take their cows "to find market," where they would be killed by men more skilled in the art of killing animals than our village butcher. The beef was sold to the hotels, to feed the tourisses.

My mother was now married to a young policeman on his way up the ladder. He drove Mr. Farmer, the Commissioner of Police, in a black Humber Hawk. My mother, as a result, was now extended credit at Goddards & Sons, on Lower Broad Street in Town.

"I can waltz-in Goddards and order anything I want and pay for it at the end o' the mont'. Lord have his mercy! You see how things does happen?"

Through this trusting or "tekking-out on account," I was introduced to the strange, new, delicious taste of "stew beef" and beef steaks. Beef was all she ever took on credit. Oh yes — and a case o' Tennents Stout!

I remember occasions when Mr. Goddard must have sold my mother English "bully beef," sneaked in amongst the Argentine beef. And when she discovered the trickery, my mother would curse Mr. Goddard, the Mother Country and all the cows in the world. The beef was so tough.

But being a woman of great improvisation, my mother developed new techniques for tenderizing any meat that was hard and tough. She would put an old rusty nail in a pot of water with the beef. If it was the season, she would pick an unripe green pawpaw from one of the trees in our backyard and scrape out the seeds; then she would slice half of the pawpaw and dump it in the boiling pot. Miraculously, the beef would melt in our mouths! Nowadays, with the progress of time, you can put ice-cubes in the saucepan after the original water has boiled out. Plain ice-cubes!

But back to our braising beef. If you're feeding four mouths, you need at least four pieces o' braising beef, each about six to eight inches long. If you think your two hips is already too nice and fat and big, you still have to admit that, when it comes to braising beef, the best pieces is the ones that have-on a lil fat and that have-in bones. One piece o' braising beef should have from three to four rib bones. The bones have-in marrow. You don't want to be known as a person who don't put no marrow in your cooking, and with no marrow in your life! And the fat going add to the in-goodness and the flavour of the food.

Wash the braising beef in warmish water with fresh lemon or lime juice squeezed in. Use either half o' lime or a whole lemon. Rub the lemon peth or the lime peth over the bones and dry off the beef on a towel. (The peth is another name for a piece o' lemon or a piece o' lime that have all its juice already squeeze-out.) Put it in a baking pan.

Cut up a onion, two sticks o' green onion, two cloves o' garlic and three sticks o' fresh parsley. Add a dash o' salt, lots o' black pepper and some brown sugar. The best way to season the braising beef is to rub-in all these ingrease-ments into the meat, *with your two hands*. That way, the seasoning will work throughout the meat, like vibrations of love.

Add a little oil to the pan and put it in the oven to broil. Pre-heat the oven by turning it to broil beforehand, because you're not baking the braising beef, you only browning it. Broil the braising beef for about fifteen minutes on each side; this will burn off most o' the fat and seize-up the marrow in the bones. When she have a nice brown colour, take it out o' the oven.

As this braising beef is cooling off — and you don't really want it to cool off, you just giving yourself time to think 'bout the next step — prepare the liquid for the sauce, which going have a curry-base. Slice up one onion, two garlic cloves and some fresh hot pepper, and add them along with some brown sugar to a good saucepan (meaning one made out o' iron) whose bottom is just barely covered in oil. Heat the pan, and stir the minute it gets hot. Let the onions and the cloves sawtay.

Add in two teaspoons o' good curry. You can get good Indian curry all over Toronto, Montreal, Winnipeg, New York, Brooklyn — wherever. But don't use the curry that they does sell in little glass bottles and shakers at the supermarkets, if you can help it. Instead, go down to a Indian food shop where they have curries of various hotness, from all over, that you could choose from. If you are not sure of yourself, axe the man behind the counter to help you choose one that isn't going burn out your tongue.

Sprinkle the curry over the onions and things, and stir and stir and stir. Use a medium heat, 'cause you don't want it to burn black as if you making colouring. Turn off the heat right now. Take it off the stove. You can start preparing the braising beef now.

Get a sharp knife and cut cross the braising beef, just where the rib bone end. From each length o' braising beef you should get four to six pieces, depending 'pon the length o' the meat. If you want to, you could throw-way the bone at this stage; but this would be against the best advice for cooking sweet food.

Put the saucepan with the curry and things in it back on the stove, and bring it to a boil. As she boil, add the braising beef. Stir she up, stir she round, turn she down to a low to medium heat, and put the cover on.

Now we go back to the breadfruit and potatoes, which are cook and already cool off. You need a masher, or something that does mash regular potatoes. If you don't have a masher, a large kitchen fork will do.

You need some cream, you need a little butter. And the most important thing that you need now is a real cou-cou stick, a real serious cultural relic.

Breadfruit has a thicker consistency than potatoes, so this is how you should prepare it. Put one piece of the breadfruit on a plate, mash it with your masher and scrape it into a large pot. Do the same with the next piece o' breadfruit, and the next, until you have mashed all the breadfruit. Then, mash the English potatoes, and throw them in the same pot with the breadfruit. Pour a little oil and a few spoonfuls of cream in with the breadfruit and potatoes, and start to stir, using your real cou-cou stick, or the makeshift one, like a wooden spoon.

The reason that I don't suggest you use a metal pot spoon is that it might mark up the bottom of your expensive saucepan with all the stirring you got to do. And you got a lot o' stirring to do! But mark you: be cautious with the amount o' cream you pour in. Yuh don't want too much, to turn the breadfruit to pap!

Turn and turn, stir and stir the mashed breadfruit and potatoes until you get them mixed into a nice paste. Put the saucepan on a low to medium heat and add in the pig tails. Start stirring from the bottom, going round and round from the side of the saucepan. Your wrist is going cry out. Breadfruit cou-cou is more tougher and strenuous to stir than corn meal cou-cou.

But stir on. Stir and stir and stir until the consistency in the pot is to your liking. If it's too dry, add a little more cream and stir. If it feel too "tight," and you still have mashed potatoes and sliced breadfruit left back, add in a little more and stir.

When you are satisfied; when the contents is smooth; when the colour is a nice light yellow or cream; when you can see the little pieces o' pig tails punctuating the bread-fruit, then you know she done. You just made breadfruit cou-cou!

At this stage, check the braising beef. Give it a last stir to make sure it not sticking to the pot, and reduce the heat to a mere simmer. You should have a lovely, thick, rich gravy. Put the lid back on the pot.

Since breadfruit cou-cou with braising beef is a heavy meal, you won't need much to eat with it. Barbadians would eat sweet potato with it; but real Wessindian sweet pota-toes would just add more starch, with the breadfruit and English potatoes. And yuh don't want all this damn starch in one meal!

I would cook the kind o' potatoes that North Amurcans does call yams. They have-in starch too, but they have a pretty colour! Put a few o' those yams in a pot of boiling water. Just before they get soft, turn off the heat, pour off the water and keep them covered.

When they have cool off a bit, they done cook. Hold one at a time in a damp towel and, using a sharp, small knife, cut off the two ends. Put the knife blade under the skin and, with a flick o' the wrist, take off the skin. Only the skin.

Cut each yam in two or three, at a slant. Put a little but-ter or olive oil in a saucepan over a low heat, and add the slice yams with a sprinkle of parsley flakes to it. Stir care-fully, and add a dash o' ground cloves or nutmeg; and stir.

You could also make a prickle to go with this meal.

Get a small bowl and put a touch o' butter in it. Scoop

out two pot spoons o' breadfruit cou-cou and put them in the bowl with the butter. Twirl-round the bowl until the breadfruit cou-cou forms itself into a smooth ball. Place the ball on a large plate and, using a spoon, make a little round indentation, like a crater, in the centre of the ball. This crater is to hold the gravy.

Breadfruit cou-cou must be eaten with a hearty amount o' gravy. Round the cou-cou, place the braising beef. At the side of the plate, place the yams and a spoonful o' prickle.

And, whilst you eating this food, Lord God, you are bound to remember poor Cap'n Bligh, sailing round the Cape o' Good Hope with the waves and wind brekking-up his ship, the HMS *Bounty*, and the sailors fighting and quarrelling, and the slaves in chains, and some o' them dying and being toss overboard. And you bound to have pity on them sailors who suffer so much and quarrel and kill one another — and who wasn't so lucky as the slaves back in the Wessindies, who didn't know how the breadfruit trees get to Barbados but who, at that time o' slavery, could still siddown and, like you this evening, enjoy a plate o' mellow breadfruit cou-cou with braising beef.

Killing a Pig to Make Pork Chops with Onions and Sweet Peppers

A pork chop? Man, you know what a real pork chop is? Or look like? A pork chop is held in such high regard in Barbados that it is one of the national symbols of the country! A pork chop is a thing that does come in any size or shape. But regardless of the size or the shape, a pork chop that is worth its salt have to have two essential characteristics: number one, it have to got-on fat; and number two, it got to have-on skin.

Christ, man, there is three things, now that I come to think about it, not two! Fat, I already mention. Skin, I mention that, too. Number three is, that a pork chop worth its name have to have-in a bone — yes, a bone, which you can suck as if the bone is a lingering, lolling candy. Anybody who hasn't walked through the roads and the lanes in a neighbourhood, chewing a pork chop bone for at least two hours, is a person who was deprived of a happy childhood.

Without these three unsubstitutable elements, a pork chop is nothing more than an ordinary piece o' meat.

I just love a pork chop. And you will too, when you try cooking a pork chop the way I am about to tell you.

In Barbados, pork is the name given to anything that is sweet. It is even a term of endearment when used to refer to a certain part of the human female anatomy, or when used to refer to anything regarding sensuality. And for good reason.

A pork chop is one of the two most sweetest and possibly one of the two most dangerous meats in the whole world. It is dangerous to people who have hang-ups about health and heart attacks and cholesterol, and who make notes about the calories they eat in everything that goes into their mouths; and to people who are frighten that they going drop dead from eating fat.

I respect their suspiciousness about a pork chop. But Barbadians is people who like to eat pork in any shape or form; who like to eat a lot, and feel that eating-off all the food is a mark of respect to their host; and who feel that you should eat everything that is put before you, because if God want you to be dead at a certain preordained time, then whether you eat pork chops that have-on fat and skin and bone or pork chops that are lean, you will still drop dead "when the Roll is called up Yonder."

If you come from a culture where the easiest thing to get and the most prevalent thing to eat is pork, you won't have many reservations about pork chops.

Pork chops? Man, gimme a pork chop first thing in the morning when I open my two eyes, even before I say a few words in prayer to God for sparing my life. And the last thing before I close my two eyes at night, gimme another pork chop!

Years and years ago, in the bygone days of courting, there were public dances in Barbados that we call brams. Brams were held in the Steel Shed in Queen's Park in Town, and there a man could meet a woman and put some sweet talk on she. And if she look good and dress good, and if she could dance good and she like dancing close, then the *only* other thing that that man had to do, in his anticipation of the sweetness to come, and in the sweet smell of her Evening-in-Paris perfume, which send him into shivers and ecstasies — the only thing was to offer the young lady *one* thing. Not a Coke nor a beer nor a ice cream. Not even a Cadbury chocolate bar nor a pack o' Wrigley's chewing gum. He would offer the lady a pork chop. A pork chop! If he didn't offer she a pork chop, the whole o' Barbados by nine o'clock the next morning would hear from the lady's lips what "a cheap, stinking son of a bitch" he was.

His cheapness and lack o' cultural sensitivity would ring throughout the neighbourhood, like church bells calling men and women to Communion.

"He dance with me, the bastard, all night. He hold me so close to him. Close, close, close. So close that I could feel even his tom-pigeon sticking me between my two legs. And when the music stop, and I had dance myself into a sweat, and sweat-up the new silk dress that I buy on time from the Indians down in Swan Street, he begin playing, the bastard, that he walking off. He not stanning his hand, to offer to buy me not even a soft drink. I seeing and tasting in my mind one o' them lovely, juicy, oily pork chops that they was selling at the bar, and that have-on such a nice, crispy ring o' skin with the fat underneat', and with a bone that I imagine myself sucking whilst I am waiting for the next set to begin. All this pass during the intermission. Intermission come and nearly gone. That bastard! What was I to think, otherwise? What? He treating me so? That bastard? And still wanting me to dance with him a second time? What the arse he take me for?"

The price of a pork chop sold at a bram was one shilling. The pork chop was golden brown and crispy and hot with fire. It was served plain, by itself, on a piece o' brown paper that quickly became soggy from the grease. The pork chop oozed in its magnificent gloriousness with the lard oil in which it was fried — and it was *always* fried. A Barbadian pork chop worth its name, like one of those sold at a bram, is always fried.

The only thing you could get to eat with this pork chop at a bram was hot sauce, which was handed to you in its bottle. The sauce was yellow from the turmeric, one of its ingreasements, and it had a hotness that would tear out your guts when you poured more than a dab on top of one of those pork chops. You can buy the same hot sauce that we used at brams even today from any Wessindian store: Windmill Pepper Sauce, which is made in Barbados.

No two pork chops sold at a bram were the same size or shape. Nor were any two pork chops served in any home in Barbados identical. I am always puzzled and intrigued when I buy pork chops in North Amurcan supermarkets. *All* the pork chops in the same package are almost identical in shape and size, as if they came out of the same mould. Not the pork chops in Barbados, not the ones cut by the neighbourhood "butcher."

All o' we, his customers down all the years, had to put up with his lack of sophistication and individualistic manner towards cutting up a pig into parts. Perhaps if our village butcher had been exposed to butchering schools and manuals and books of instruction, which are so popular and available in these modern days, and perhaps if he hadn't become indignant and start cursing stink-stink when told of a required curriculum of butchering, he might have acquired a little more finesse and "niceness" about the way he cut up a sow pig or a boar hog.

The tools of butchers in those days comprised a knife that was sharp and long, a knife that was sharp and short, and a sharpening stone. The long knife, sometimes more than eight inches in length, and thinner from the hilt down to the tip, was for sticking the pig. It was long enough to pierce the neck, penetrate the thick throat, and touch the heart or some other critical part of the pig's insides. The short knife was for "butchering-up" or cutting-up the pig.

Armed with these three implements, the tools of his profession, all the butcher had to do was wait until some woman summon him and ask him to come and kill her pig, please, next Saturday.

"I have a pig to kill," she tell him, "and I want you to kill it for me."

The butcher would not display, by his manner of response, any excitement at having suddenly been raised from the ranks of the underemployed. He would probably regard this engagement as just a mild assault upon his leisure, an unnecessary intrusion that he resented. It was an interruption of his concentration upon the interminable playing of dominoes, or cards, or throwing dice. He was a man who would just sit and sharpen his knives while waiting for the next customer. But the woman with the pig to be killed would want him to put more enthusiasm and seriousness into her engaging his services.

"Is next Saturday. Hear? I have a lot o' customers depending on me. Including the Plantation."

This communication, through local custom, had to be delivered by the woman with the pig, in person, at least one week in advance. She might also have to "warm his palm

with a little something," a down payment on his services —
not because his talent and services were demanded so often,
but just as a symbol in the matter of respect. He might be
the only man in the neighbourhood, the only man for miles
around, in possession of, and armed with, two sharpened
knives. And you wouldn't want to have to walk to another
district and let a stranger know your business — that you
were killing a pig — and have the whole population of
strangers from that village congregate in your backyard
asking for this piece and that piece, and wanting to buy
your pork on credit.

"When I catch my hand in a week or two, you is the
first body I intend to pay."

Oh, no! Not before you give your regular customers
the part that they want, that they reserved while you was
deciding when is the best Saturday to kill your pig. Oh, no!
After all, you won't be so foolish as to kill your pig on the
same day that another woman in another neighbourhood
was killing hers. Oh, no! That ain't sense!

So, for days after the woman who own the pig make the
appointment, if you was to walk near the butcher's house
or venture through the gate in his paling, you would see
him bending over a piece o' black stone, passing his blade
over it in an unending circular motion, sharpening the long
knife and the short knife. And he would then practise the
keenness of the two knives on a piece o' newspaper or on
a cane blade. And during the week preceding the Saturday
of the killing, the butcher would pass round by the woman's

house to investigate the pig: size it up, gauge how heavy it is, weigh it in his mind and plan his attack.

"Just the same way," my mother tell me one dark night, telling ghost stories, when the wind howl through the jalousies, and make the jalousies and my teeth rattle, "just the same as hengman up at Glandairy Prison does-do!"

She lowered her voice, and the night became more blacker and eerie.

"Watch!" she say, "as the hengman sneaking near the cell of the condemn' man, sizing up the heaviness of his weight and the shirt size of his neck, and other things essential to the knowledge a good hengman have to have. Look, boy, how he does study *all* these things about that poor condemn' man: how he does walk, how he does move, how he does stannup. All these lil details."

Suddenly there is no wind. There is no moon shining. There is only the blackness.

"And when the day o' reckoning for the condemn' man come, *bram!*" I nearly had a heart-affection. "One time! His neck brek!"

The butcher would pay doomsday visits to estimate the pig's size and weight, and to figure out how much heavier the pig was going to be as dead weight and how much heavier compared to his own weight. He would have to decide whether he would need an assistant, some idle boy from the village to help him with the dirtier, heavier work.

"'Cause a big, fat pig like this could be trouble," the butcher thinks, "if it weigh more than a man. And in case

I should take a lil sip o' grog to settle my nerves. 'Cause there is pigs that in my lifetime in this village weighed more than the best butcher!"

At the same time as the butcher continues fastidiously to sharpen his knives, the woman killing the pig (meaning the woman whose pig was to be killed) will be going through the neighbourhood, "engaging the pork." She will knock on every house, and tell every woman, except those she isn't speaking to because of some small altercation or difference of opinion, "I killing a pig this Saturday. What you want?"

"Girl," the customer say, "lemme put in a order now that you here."

"Wha' part?"

"Gimme a piece that have on a little skin. And a bone. I don't know yet what I making Sunday, but a piece with the skin would suit."

"Near the head, or near the end?"

"Once it have on skin, girl, I don't mind."

"Thanks." And off to another house to hear its order, to engage the pig.

This next woman is quarrelsome. She didn't like what she got the last time, and an emotional argument erupts.

"All these blasted years," she tell her, "you been killing pigs, and all these years I been ordering from you, and all these years you never ever shown me the courtesy or the decency to give me what I axe for, exactly. Last three months when you was killing a pig, I particular axe you for a piece o' pork near the hind legs. I had in mind to bake the thing with lil dry-peas and rice. Be-Christ, when I on-wrapped the paper you send it in and I see what you had the nerve to send to me, using *your* preferences and not *mine*, I had to say to myself, 'Beryl, 'twas a time when I couldda depend on Gertrude to send me the piece o' pork I order. But since Gertrude killing pigs more regular, and getting on in the world, she not noticing her old-time cus-tomers.' You only satisfying them that live in more bigger house than me. And the people who live over there — the Plantation House! But Gertrude, I telling you this for the last time: I want a piece o' pork that near the leg, and that got on lil bone, and skin naturally. To bake. To bake on Sunday. You hear? Now, don't let me have to lose my blasted crosses with you again!"

Gertrude uses her lips to wet the tip of a lead pencil, and writes, in her neat, careful hand, this new order in the exercise book she's borrowed from one of her children. She knows that her reputation stands in the scales in which she will weigh her pork.

"But Beryl, you didn't tell me hommuch. A pung? A pung and a half?"

"Put me down for two pungs, girl!"

Gertrude does not tell her customer everything, though. She neglects a very important detail: that she is making black pudding and souse on the same Saturday. She, as every woman in the neighbourhood knows, is "keeping the head for herself."

The head of the pig is required for the making of souse, and the "belly" (the entrails or intestines) is used to make the black pudding. Pig feet are the choice parts for making souse. The pig — her pig, any pig, all pigs — has only four feet to be divided amongst all the favoured, dependable mouths in the neighbourhood; so, the making of pudding and souse must be kept quiet. The secret must be divulged only to the best people, whose status have absolutely nothing at all to do with the amount o' money in their pocket. Their status have only to do with their class in the neighbourhood.

Gertrude has her favourite customers, and these women she will ask in a conspiratorial whisper, "Pudding and souse? Hommuch you ordering?" She won't sell a woman even one ounce of pork on Saturday if that woman does not, when told about it, intend to order also some black pudding and souse.

So Gertrude's exercise book with its ruled lines gets more entries and is soon full-up with orders. She does not stop walking until the last piece of pork is engaged. And she must not forget that the butcher has to get a piece, which he is permitted to choose, because of his status as the person killing the pig.

The Friday night before the killing, the shop full-up with women buying groceries for the weekend, including Gertrude. The butcher, passing for a snap o' rum and to chat with his teasing men-friends, shows her his long knife and his short knife, for reassurance, and reminds her that he will need a wooden table laid out in the yard.

"If not a wooden table," he advise her, "a sheet o' three-ply, propp-up on two horses, will do. And lots of hot, boiling water, and a large bucket for the blood and the belly. And how we going dispose and get rid o' the guts and the bowels?"

Gertrude's own reputation is in the balance.

"Don't worry-out your soul case, boy. I have everything shipshape. All you got to do is show up. You come. Come five 'clock in the morning and kill the blasted pig. I have people like anything on this piece o' paper you see in my hand, wanting a piece o' my pork. So, you come. I don't even know if I feed the pig properly and fatten-she-up enough to satisfy the orders I have for a piece o' pork in the morning."

Jokes then rise in the merry shop, and men tease the butcher and remind him of that last time in the recent history of the neighbourhood, four Saturdays ago, when a pig he was trying to kill slipped out o' his hands and escaped. The pig fled through a field o' green sugar cane, and never was found!

"Do not," they warn him, "do not let this next pig got-'way from you! Not before you have stick the pig in the right place! Hear?"

The butcher sharpens his long knife and his short knife in silent embarrassment as the men drink another grog on his head, in his honour, all of which he has to pay for.

"To you, man! And to the pig tomorrow morning! Down the hatch!"

Everything is now fixed and ready for the killing.

In the backyard is the wooden table. The butcher will use it to put the pig on, to cut it up on. The water to be boiled is in large buckets, or in discarded oil drums; and floating in the water, like lilies in a pond, are leaves freshly cut from a tree — probably a clammy-cherry tree. The leaves keep the water fresh and clean, and prevent it from falling out of the buckets or drums when they are carried from the public standpipe, by hand or by donkey-cart, to the yard. A cloth covers each bucket and drum, for cleanliness. Flies are droning about like Spitfires.

The wood for fuel has been brought in. Gertrude will need lots of wood to boil the cauldrons of water. She has one pail in which to collect the blood, one for the belly, one for the offal, and still another for the harslick and the "light." She has a large basin or two in which to place the parts of the pig that the butcher is going to cut up, and she has a lot of sand or fine marl or sawdust to spread around the killing area to absorb the blood and the parts of the guts that may fall off the table.

Her exercise book with its ruled pages is spread out, showing the orders she has collected. The most important order is from the Plantation House. This one she has underlined in red. This one she will fill first.

"THE PLANTATION HOUSE," her entry reads, in capital

letters. "10 PUNGS OF THE BEST PORK. A JOINT FOR SUN-
DAY LUNCH. AND TEN SHILLINGS IN SOUSE, LOTS OF GRIZ-
ZLE. IF POSSIBLE, GRIZZLE ONLY. SOUSE TO BE MAINLY
PIG FOOTS. NO BLACK PUDDING BECAUSE OF THE BLOOD
AND THE COLOUR. WHITE PUDDING ONLY."

Is Saturday morning. Gertrude up long before the butcher,
long before the birds, long before the wood-doves up in the
mahogany trees start their cooing to welcome in the dawn.
Gertrude already said her prayers, remembering to ask
God for some kind o' mercy and luck today, 'cause she sell
more pork in her exercise book than the weight of the pig
in the pen could provide. Oh, loss! She ask God also for
absolution because she have to kill this pig, which she had
start to like bad, bad, bad, and uses to bathe sometimes two
times a day.

"But God, you understand," she entreats.

The butcher is punctual. Is still dark dark. The house
ain't got in no electricity, so they using lanterns. Dogs,
smelling danger and raw pork and blood, been barking all
night, as if they expect that the butcher's long knife will
make a lil slip, a error, and land at their throats instead. The
barking follows the progress of the butcher as he enters the
yard dressed in a black jacket, a pair of black trousers rolled
up above his bare feet and ankles, and a felt hat that was not
black when it was new but is black now. His black clothes
suit his profession. He is in the same league as the hengman
at Her Majesty's Prison at Glandairy.

"I here, Mistress!" the butcher call out. And these are the last words that will pass his lips. From the moment he grabs the hind legs of the pig and wraps thick rope round them and does the same thing with the front legs, like a cowboy roping a bucking horse, the pig is screeching.

"*Eeeeeeeennnk!*"

The pig knows its plight and struggles to postpone its day of reckoning, looking in the direction of Gertrude, its owner, who turns her eyes away.

Remembering his own recent history with slippery pigs, the butcher makes sure that the rope is tight and strong. He fills his lungs with the fresh air of dawn and of bougain-villeas, and with wafts of smoke from canes burnt the night before, and hefts the huge boar hog out of its pen, slings it over his shoulder, bends a little from the weight (which he has not guessed correctly), stumbles a little, wavers and, like a drunken man, moves uncertainly to the middle of the yard, where the large wooden table stands like the platform of a gallows.

The butcher throws the screaming pig onto its back on the table. In the weak light of the breaking dawn, he pulls the sharpened long knife from some part of his black cloth-ing, and in a flash silences the anger and protests of the pig whose sudden silence matches the butcher's own voiceless concentration.

Hot water is immediately poured over the pig, so that its black silken hairs are easier to scrub off from its pink-white thick skin with a stone. When this is done, and the pig's colour has changed from black to almost white to pink, the butcher takes his sharp short knife from the table and draws a thin line across the belly of the pig. Onto the table tumble the guts and those unimaginable things from within the stomach in a greenish unrolling of tubes that slither. Gertrude turns her face away. She makes the sign of the cross and says, "Jesus Christ."

The butcher is still silent and methodical. He starts cutting up the flesh into pieces, hacking off any part of the pig in any way, according to whim and fancy, and to suit the desire of the customers. He will cut up the pig to the last bone to suit any impulse, and therefore not in the anatomically strict manner in which butchers in Canada and Amurca, graduates of some authorized pig-butchering course who follow a diagram, are schooled to do.

When Gertrude becomes strong enough to face the blood and the entrails and the transformation of her "pet," the butcher has already chopped off the legs, the head is severed from the rest of the body, and the blood is caught in a pail.

Gertrude begins to clean the head, rubbing its snout and its ears and its eyes with a stone and with sand to remove the bristles of hair. The liver and the light are placed in their own pan.

The butcher offers her the pig feet. "These going make some lovely souse," he says. And his voice in the darkness frightens her. These are the first words that have passed his lips since he arrived at five o'clock. It is now ten o'clock.

Butchering takes time. These first few words the butcher has spoken remind Gertrude of church, of sin, of blood. They sound like the vicar giving benediction. They make her jump a little, they come at her so surprisingly. And then she smiles. The worst is over.

You will not easily be able to buy a real Barbadian pork chop in Canada or Amurca, unless you go to Brooklyn, New York, and somebody takes you to Princess Place or Peggy Place. They ain't got no place like that in Toronto. But if you know the butcher in the meat store where you does frequent, he might be able to cut you a pork chop to almost match the cut a Barbadian butcher would hack off.

Have him give you a cut with a bit of skin on it. If he can't do this for whatever reason, perhaps due to health regulations, ask for a cut with a thin strip of fat. And of course, it should have a bone in it.

Some butchers would cut you a pork chop that is about one pound. I can't guess weights, but a big pork chop, about a inch to a inch and a half thick, would be the preferable size and thickness, respectively.

Wash the two pork chops (if you are feeding two persons) in warm water and dry them off. Put them in a pan and squeeze some lemon juice on each side. Leave them in the lemon juice for a few minutes. Then wipe off the excess lemon juice.

The tools you need now are a sharp knife and a spoon. The ingreasements you need for the dressing, or seasoning, are black pepper, salt, garlic cloves, nutmeg, a large onion, green onions and a large sweet pepper, either red or green. If you're concerned about the aesthetics o' colour in your food, choose a red sweet pepper. The onion could be one of those big red ones, simply because you going to use only one large slice on each pork chop; a slice of a big red onion would almost coincide with the size of the pork chop.

Turn the oven on to 350 degrees. These pork chops that you cooking not going be fried, like the pork chops at the Queen's Park brams. I eat hardly anything that is fried.

Chop up two stems o' green onions fine-fine-fine. Press two cloves o' garlic and add them to the green onions, along with a few sprigs of fresh thyme. Grind these ingreasements into a paste by rolling a bottle over them on the counter or 'pon a piece a board, like a cutting-board. More modern cooks would put these ingreasements in a blender, but they going get the same results. A mortar and pestle would do an even better job.

Now, you get the sharp knife and punch holes through the thickness or the sides of the pork chops. Push about half a teaspoonful of the ground-up seasoning into each hole. A pork chop, even if it is not as large as a Barbadian pork chop, should have four holes, at the most, for putting the seasoning in. If the pork chop have skin on it, you can pierce the skin and fill the hole with the seasoning.

Naturally, you have to use a pinch o' salt and one dash or two dash o' black pepper in the seasoning that you ground up. But it doesn't matter if you forgot to do this;

you could always sprinkle the pork chops with salt and black pepper now, at this juncture. And sprinkle a lil sugar on each side of the pork chops as well. You could use white sugar. Brown sugar might darken the pork chops tummuch and make it difficult for you to tell whether they cook properly.

If you still insist on frying these pork chops, then you could use brown sugar, and if you want to make style, use Demerara brown sugar. You will also need a light batter. Mix a little flour with breadcrumbs, thoroughly; and with your two hands, slap it onto the pork chops. Put the pork chops in a hot — but not too hot — pan. Once they are cooked through, transfer them to a plate. In the same pan fry some slices o' onion and sweet pepper.

But the pork chops we been discussing is pork chops to be baked. They've been stuffed with the seasoning and sprinkled with a dash of salt, black pepper and white sugar. Put a little oil in the bottom of a baking pan and add the pork chops to the pan. Place a slice o' onion on each pork chop, and then place a ring o' sweet pepper on each one, making sure that the sweet pepper, if possible, have a larger circumference than the onion. If this is not possible, don't worry; just place the sweet pepper 'pon top the onion.

The oven should be preheated by now. So, put the pork chops in the oven. After the first fifteen minutes, take the pork chops out and baste them with the same juice that is in the baking pan. Remove the onion and the sweet pepper while you doing this, then replace them on top of the chops before you put-back the chops in the oven. You may baste the pork chops two more times before they done cooking.

If for some reason you fear that the onion and the sweet peppers going get barbecued instead of being baked, you can always take them out and keep them warm as the pork chops are being baked. When the pork chops are golden brown, turn the oven off, and replace the onions and peppers on top the chops before serving them. Then pour the gravy, which is made automatically in the baking pan, over the pork chops.

This is a rich meal, so you had better serve it with plain rice. A slice of sweet potato beside each pork chop will make a pleasant combination. If you concerned with the aesthetics of food, serve yams instead of the Wessindian sweet potato. Wessindian sweet potato is more white in colour than North Amurcan yam, and starchier.

There is nothing to say that you can't serve carrots. But parboil them or scald them first; and when the pork chops start to make a gravy in the baking pan, then add the carrots. The results going be real sweet food.

I going to depart from custom and suggest a salad for this meal. I doing this 'cause you cook these pork chops in the winter, and on a cold day you need something more, something that is going to stick to your ribs and clothe you in a warmth of gastronomical satisfaction.

Make a salad of spinach leaves and lettuce. In this case, iceberg lettuce will not be too bad. I suggest you add a few spring tomatoes and a generous portion o' fresh parsley to the lettuce. To add a tantalizing zing to this salad, crumble up a little blue cheese, which must be firm and dry. A touch o' white sugar, lemon juice and olive oil add to the bowl, gently mix together, and *bram!* you are off to the races.

And now that you eat these baked pork chops, Bajan style, a lil thing like a screeling pig five o' clock any Saturday morning, with its shrillness of torment and impending doom, could hardly affect your sensibilities.

When your teeth bite into that pork chop, and you taste the skin, you will go straight back to those brams in the Queen's Park Shed in Barbados, and imagine you is the man at the bram, buying a pork chop for the woman you have on your mind; or that you is the woman, eating all this sweet goodness. A Bajan pork chop.

Souse
(but no black pudding)

Some people does live only for Sundays. To go to church. Some people does live only for Fridays. Pay-day. Some people does live for Wednesdays. To attend mid-week church or to go to Mothers Union meetings, or just because Wednesday is soup day.

But with me? Gimme Saturdays any morning. Gimme Saturdays seven days of the week! Saturday, when I was growing up, was the day for making black pudding and souse, the best food in the world. As a young, strapping teenager, the race-horse, as my mother called me, I used to walk across half o' the island o' Barbados: from Paynes Bay in Sin-James parish, where I was living at the time, right up to the Abbey in Christ Church parish, a journey of twelve miles at least. And when you realize that Barbados is twenty-one miles in the longest straightest direction, you *know* how long twelve miles is, out o' twenty-one! Just to get pudding and souse.

Up in the Abbey there was the Kings, a whole family o' girls who could make some o' the sweetest pudding and souse in the whole island. To-besides, one of the King girls was in love with me.

But whether or not you was in love, you still would make sure that the woman you eating pudding and souse from was a clean person — clean enough that you could close your two eyes and eat a piece o' snout, or a piece o' the ear, and not feel funny. Yuh know? From childhood you was taught to-don't eat black pudding and souse from any-and-everybody who makes it, you hear? Some people don't clean the belly and the pig feets clean-clean, yuh!

"Watch what going into your stomach, boy!"

So, from reputation, word o' mouth, and because you know the woman who make the black pudding and souse (she and your mother might be friends), you would track she down to the ends o' the earth, just to "taste her hand" on a Saturday. The reputation of the best makers o' pudding and souse does spread through the whole island, and men does travel from Sin-Lucy parish in the north to Oistin's Town in Christ Church in the south, *just* to taste that woman's hand.

But travelling all that distance to eat black pudding and souse, walking for miles and miles in the damn hot sun if you don't have a bicycle, is not merely to full-up your belly with pig foots and snout and pieces of ear. Eating black pudding and souse on a Saturday is a social event, with certain protocols that go with it, certain rites and rituals. For example, if you buying the pudding and souse in a rum shop, you have to buy a rum first. If you buying it from a pudding-and-souse woman, you first have to engage her in conversation. Axe she 'bout her thrildren (her children), or her boyfriend if you's the same age as she. And only when them pleasantries are finish, then you can tell she, "Child, gimme some o' this nice pudding and souse!"

In Brooklyn, where there is more Barbadians than the sum total o' Barbadians living in Barbados, the pudding and souse comes in strict political stripes. Lemme explain what this mean.

Pudding and souse, as you remember, is the national dish o' Barbados. The Barbadian national pastime is talking 'bout politics. And since eating pudding and souse is something that you does do in a rum shop, whilst you're talking — and "talking a lotta shite" as we say, meaning talking about politics, church, women, men and thrildren — it is a case o' night following the day that, whilst sucking on a pig foot, you might be hearing about the Barbadian budget, the latest political scandal in Barbados, hearing who really kill Mark Stokes and drop he in the sea, or if a certain prime minister o' Barbados dead from drugs or from poisoning, or if a woman kill he, in truth. So, eating pudding and souse in a rum shop is a dangerous pastime.

In Barbados there are three political parties: the Democratic Labour Party (the Dems); the Barbados Labour Party (the Bees); and a third party (trying to survive), the New Democratic Party (the NDP). Now, in Brooklyn it may happen (as it does happen) that the woman making the pudding and souse is a supporter — and I don't mean just a ordinary supporter, I mean a *staunch* supporter, a member, a party woman — of one of the political parties back in Barbados. If you don't support the same party, don't try entering her place to buy a piece o' souse! Find someplace else that does sell pudding and souse.

There are two women of "substantial consequence," as my mother say, down in Brooklyn, New York, who does make pudding and souse: Peggy and Princess. I hear that Peggy is a supporter of the Bees; Princess is a supporter of the Dems. I hear so. Don't mix up your politics and neither Peggy nor Princess will mix up your pudding and souse. Not that Peggy won't serve you if you is a member of the Dems; but you might not feel too good eating a yard o' black pudding in the political stronghold of the enemy. Some fellers who is members o' the Dems does feel just as comfortable eating a pig foot cook by a Bees supporter, but these in the minority.

With Princess, if you don't show your stripes, forget it.

"Don't kiss-me-arse trespass, then!" Princess will tell yuh. "Leff! Or stand-home!"

Souse

When I was a boy, every Saturday afternoon as God send, around two o'clock, the hottest part of the afternoon, you would see a woman sitting down by the door of the neighbourhood shop, Miss Edwards's Shop, behind a big tray placed on a box. The large cloth covering the tray, and protecting its contents from flies, was made from a flour bag that was bleached for days and days until the red and blue names of the Canadian mill and manufacturer disappeared and the cloth became white as snow.

The woman sat on a smaller box as if it were a throne. She wore a starched and ironed dress that had white flowers in the design, and her white apron was starched and pleated, reaching below her knee. Her hair was combed back severely from her forehead in corn rows and tied tightly with a white ribbon.

This is the black-pudding-and-souse woman. A goddess. A Queen of Hot-Cuisine, Bajan style. The High Priestess o' Souse!

If she didn't have a good reputation throughout the whole neighbourhood, and if she wasn't a woman that pass muster, cleanliness-wise and decency-wise, she could sit for days and days on end offering people black pudding and souse free, and not one soul would take even a half-inch o' pudding or one little piece o' souse from her tray. But the fact that this woman sitting down there, beside the door of the shop, where all the neighbours buy their groceries, in full daylight, in all her starched white and hair-greased majesty, mean that she is somebody important, somebody accepted, somebody clean in the neighbourhood. Her place is secure and sanctified.

The fact that she selling black pudding and souse, and that you happen to have money in your pocket, don't mean that you could fork yourself up to her tray and say, "Gimme five shillings in pudding and souse!" You just do not tell *her* what you want and what you don't want. Oh, no! You would have to take what *she* give you, even though it is your money buying it.

Back there and back then, money didn't do the same kind o' talking that money does do up here in Canada and Amurca. Oh, no! Before money, you have to have the class to go with it; 'cause a lot o' other people in the neighbourhood have class, and more class than you. Oh, yes! So, without class, you have to wait your turn.

"And know your blasted place, boy!" the black-pudding-and-souse woman would tell you. And she would laugh, "Heh-hehhh!" to soften the blow in the reminder.

Imagine a boy going up to this black-pudding-and-souse woman and telling she, "Gimme two shillings in souse. And I want the pig's feet and some of the ear! And three shillings in the black pudding. And I want the white black pudding, not the black black pudding!"

He would have to be born mad!

"What you say?" the black-pudding-and-souse woman would ask he. "You *want*? You want *what*? Look, nigger-man, you will get what *I* decide to sell you. What the hell you mean by 'you want'? You want a lash in your arse! Have manners, boy. I have souse put-by for the lady in the wall house, out the Front Road — one o' my steady customers. And I have to save-back ten shillings in pig's feet for the manager o' the Plantation. And Mistress Yard, out the Front Road, have to have her souse, six shillings' worth, and two yards o' the white black pudding. And you come stanning-up in front o' me, in front my tray, telling *me* you want? You want a lash in you lil black arse! Wait your turn, boy. Know your place! I could maybe spare six cents in souse, and give you a sixpence in black pudding. *Maybe*, if yuh lucky. You want it? Or you don't want it? Speak your damn mind. I busy with my regular customers!" And as she is saying, she is serving other customers.

This boy, perhaps an apprentice mechanic or a pupil-teacher, but with no more status than the few shillings rackling-'bout in his pocket, is being put in his place. The black-pudding-and-souse woman emphasizes her reprimand by telling him, "Look, boy! 'Stead o' humbugging me, and getting-on as if you don't have any manners, take this order to Mistress Luke 'cross the road. And don't shake it and throw-way the juice from the lady's souse! When you come back, I will fix you. Go!"

And he would obey.

Look at me back then, with my white short pants, three-quarter white stockings, brown-and-white John White shoes with holes of brogue in them, school blazer with school crest, and open-neck white shirt. I'm armed with a straw basket that has flowers worked into its design, and the word BARBADOS written in letters that look like the vines of the bougainvillea, in red and blue. The basket has a cover, and inside is a white Pyrex bowl with a matching cover and a linen towel to cover-down the bowl.

I'm walking 'cross the road, to stand up in front the black-pudding-and-souse woman.

"Good afternoon, Mistress Whittaker."

"Good afternoon, boy."

"My mother say to say, 'How-d' do.'"

"How-d' do?" she say to me. "How-d' do to her too! How your mother?"

"My mother well. She send me for the thing."

"I know, I know. You don't have to tell me. Your mother been tekking her stuff from me for years now, boy. Before you born. How school? You learning good?"

"I learning good, ma'am."

"Your Scriptures?"

"I learning my Scriptures good, ma'am."

"Well, that's good. Gimme the basket, if you please. You not too big to read the Good Book. You understand? Study hard, and become a man, boy. Tell your mother for me that I putting in a extra pig's foot. But she can't get none of the snout this week. I have orders like anything to full, for the Plantation today. They having a party over there. Where you playing cricket today?"

"We playing another school."

"The Alleyne Boys School wunnuh playing?"

"No, ma'am."

"Well, which, then?"

"Foundation."

"Foundation Boys? Them half o' hooligans? I hope wunnuh paint their arse with runs! Pardon my French. But them Foundation boys? They think they is men — don't shake the basket with your mother souse, boy! — I hope you make a hundred runs today, as a Cawmere Boy! Go. In the name of the Lord. You growing to be a nice young man, boy."

"Yes, ma'am. Thanks, Mistress Whittaker."

"And tell your mother, for me, that she owe me now for three Saturdays in a row. But I will see her in church at 'leven o'clock matins, bright and early tomorrow. Or at Mothers Union."

Now, to find out how black pudding and souse is made, we have to return to the big wooden table in Gertrude's backyard where the dead pig is lying.

The pig head cut off by now, and the blood collected in a pail, because some o' this blood is to be used to make the black pudding. The butcher just handed the four feet, or trotters, to Gertrude, along with pieces o' pork up by the knees, the ham hocks.

For the rest of the morning the woman will work and work, cleaning these parts o' the pig, washing them in lime juice. The biggest job is "to clean the belly" — to wash out, over and over again, all the intestines, which is the part used to make black pudding.

First, you take the intestines and empty them out. Then you clean them clean-clean-clean, and soak them in a bucket with lots o' lime juice and white vinegar. You have to find a way to turn the intestines inside-out in order to clean them even more better still. Then turn-back the insides, outside-in, and wash them some more. And some more, until they really clean.

When you finish cleaning the belly, you have to dry them off and then soak them again in lime juice, a lil salt and a lil white vinegar, and leave them to "draw." "Drawing" means that the salt and lime juice and vinegar going have a chance to work into the belly, so that the taste of "freshness" (since a pig was alive one minute, dead the next and eaten the same day) is drowned and killed.

You now have time to start peeling the sweet potatoes and grating them. You got to cut up the onions, eschalots, cucumber and fresh broad-leaf thyme into lil pieces. Cut up the hot pepper, and please, don't pass your two hands near your eyes! That pepper doesn't make sport. It real hot! Mix in a lil flour with the grated sweet potato to give it some body. Add in some nutmeg or cloves, some sugar, some salt and some hot pepper, and mix up all these in-greasements.

To make black pudding that is black, you would have to add in some blood to give colour to the mixture. But if you have bad nerves, or a weak stomach, forget the blood;

you can use food colouring instead. Or just leave the mixture as it is. Black pudding without the blood or food colouring is called white black pudding, or white pudding.

Now get a funnel, and tie the funnel to one end of a clean and dry intestine. Tie-off the other end of the intestine and start stuffing the grated potato mixture into the intestine through the funnel. You ever heard of chitlings? Well, this is how chitlings was born.

When the intestine is full-up with the potato, but not packed too tight, tie-she-off with another piece o' string. Full-up all the intestines with the potato mixture in this way, until all the grated potato been used.

If you have any intestines leff back, you could boil them or fry them by themselves. If you run out o' intestine and have some grated potato mixture leff back, throw all of this in a frying pan with hot lard oil, or olive oil, and my God in heaven! — the consequence o' frying this stuffing is bound to gladden your heart.

Food, like most things, is something that you have to improvise with. You have to use the ingreasements that are available, or that grow in your backyard. We in Barbados, where black pudding and souse was made first in 1752 — long before anybody heard o' Trinidad or Jamaica or Sin-Kitts — we uses to grow a lot o' sweet potatoes. So we does stuff the intestines with grated sweet potato.

Down in Guyana, and in some parts o' Trinidad, they never saw a real sweet potato in their lives, unless a uncle or a aunt put one in a envelope or a barrel and post it to

Port-of-Spain or Georgetown. But they have rice. So, Trinidadians and Guyanese does stuff their black pudding with rice. It don't taste too bad. You could eat it. But it ain't Bajan pudding!

Back to our intestines. They now stuffed with the grated potatoes and waiting on a large plate. Put a large — and I mean large — pot or saucepan o' water on the fire, and drop in a bay leaf or two. Bring the water to a boil. Then turn down the heat and take up each stuffed intestine careful, careful, careful in your hand, and lay she down in the water, without splashing the water. Don't cover-down the pot. You need to see what happening inside that pot.

The most important thing to remember not to do, whilst your intestines is boiling, is to talk. Do not talk. Talking is the worst thing you could do, over a pot o' black pudding that cooking.

Do not open your mouth, even to tell your boyfriend or your girlfriend that you love him or her, or to tell your husband that he is a son-of-a-bitch for not helping you clean the belly. Do not utter one word. Because to talk while your black pudding is cooking in a pot, according to the best superstitions and laws o' voodoo of Barbados, is to make the black pudding burst in the pot. The sausage casings going burst and explode, and transform the contents o' this big pot into a pool o' brown porridge.

I just give you a quick lesson in making black pudding. I wouldn't advise you to try your hand in making it, though. It's tummuch work. And too risky.

Souse, on the other hand, is different. It's made from the pig's feet, from the ham hocks, from parts o' the pig head, like the snout and the ears, and from some of the leaner parts of the pig, near the belly. These parts, or "features," are boiled until they are soft. They are either left to cool off in the water in which they were cooked, or are taken out and placed on the counter to cool, or are put in cold water to cool off quickly.

While these pig features cooling off, it's time to make the prickle. The prickle for souse is the mixture in which the features are put to soak and get "soused-up." Hence the name of the dish, souse.

Cut up onions, green onions, cucumber and fresh thyme in a large bowl. Don't slice the cucumber; dice it.

Add salt and pepper to suit your taste. Fresh hot peppers is always better than black pepper shaken from a shaker. Don't forget a touch o' white vinegar, to help the pork draw.

Stir up these ingreasements in a bowl, and taste the prickle to make sure it reach the hotness you like. Expert souse-makers does argue that you *must* pour a lil water in which the features was cooked into the prickle, to give it some body and that nice taste o' pork.

Incidentally, souse made from a pig just killed is more better and tastier than souse made from pork that you buy in a supermarket.

When the pork features cool off, clean them using a lot

o' lemon. Rub and rub lemon peth all over them. The cleaning of the features at this stage is the most important part of the preparation of souse.

Cut up the features in bite-size pieces and throw them in the prickle. Stir them round, and cover them down for at least one hour. Two hours is the correct amount of time to leave them sousing-up. The more longer they soak in the prickle, the more better they will be soused-up, and the sweeter your souse going taste.

Some people who pretend they was born in the Wessindies does put up their nose at this way of eating souse cold. They argue that souse got to be served hot and eaten *hot*. But don't mind them. Those unbelievers are Wessindians who was born in Sin-Kitts or the Bahamas. No Guyanese, nor Trinidadian nor Grenadian, would try to mislead you by telling you that souse have to be served hot.

Souse, the real Barbadian souse, *have* to be served and eaten one way only: cold.

Another thing that you might hear from some Wessindians is that anyone who does consume blood in their food, from an animal, have cannibalistic tendencies. Well, I am not going tell you that I like pig blood in my black pudding. Nor am I *not* going tell you that I do not like blood in my black pudding. Historically and culturally speaking, there is two kinds o' black pudding: black pudding that is black and black pudding that is white.

Now that the features soaking, you have time to pour yourself a beer or a rum and soda, or better still, a Bajan rum punch. And whilst you are sipping that rum punch take out the lengths o' black pudding from the pot and lay them on a large platter.

Dip a piece o' paper towel, or even better, a few feathers tied together to make a light brush, in some olive oil, lard oil or any kind o' oil, and brush it over each piece o' black pudding as if you're touching up a water-colour painting. Light and nice. You are going to see the black pudding shine like a first-class Polish sausage.

When you ready to serve, this is how you do it. Get a sharp knife and cut off pieces o' black pudding, about two inches in length. Put a couple of pieces on a plate with a few pieces o' souse, consisting of a pig foot, a piece o' the ear, the snout, and a nice piece from the ham hock. Pour a lil prickle all over the souse, and sprinkle a few pieces of fresh parsley or watercress on the black pudding. You could add some fresh parsley to the souse to make it look pretty, or as North Amurcans would say, to "garnish" it.

There is a special way, ordain in Barbadian culture and history, of eating pudding and souse. You eat it out in the open air, in the hot sun, with the sea breeze blowing in your face and the wind licking your body.

If you don't eat-off all the souse and black pudding the same day it made, then have it for breakfast the next morning. All you have to do is fry the black pudding in a pan with a lil butter; not with too much heat, though. And you can fry-up the souse too. But don't pour in the prickle with the souse when you frying it. (Real Barbadians would know how to cut up pieces of the souse, small-small, mix them in flour, and fry them to make "souse-fritters.")

Serve this meal o' pudding and souse with some fresh bread, but no butter, as you would if you were serving it on Saturday.

So, this is pudding and souse, the food of the gods and of the slaves of Barbados.

Black pudding and souse would have to be the ultimate in slave food. It is made from the parts of the pig that nobody else wanted or had the heart to eat. But regardless, pudding and souse is the sweetest thing handed down by our ancestors, African slaves, to each and every one of us present-day Wessindians.

Perhaps it is a dish that you would have to be born in the particular culture that prepares it for you to understand and appreciate it. If you taste it once, you bound to want to taste it every Saturday for the rest of your life.

A lot o' people does talk about it, but few can make it. In other words, the Biblical saying can be applied to the making of pudding and souse: "Many are called, but few are chosen."

When you meet a woman who does make sweet pudding and souse, you will make sure that you keep her as a friend, as a wife or as a lover for the rest o' your life, the rest o' your born days.

The next time you see a black-pudding-and-souse woman, you tell she, "I would like a lil pudding and souse."

"How you want it?" she going ask you.

"Man, put it in my hand, man! And don't forget to pour some of the prickle . . ."

She going cut you a inch o' black pudding that is black and a inch o' black pudding that is white, and place them on a sheet o' brown paper. She going pass the feathers dipped in oil over the black pudding. And you going eat-off these two pieces fast fast because the pudding sweet, oh my God in heaven! It too sweet, in-true! And then the real sport going begin.

"You tekking your souse now, then?" she going axe you.

And with her ladle she going stir up all that sweet prickle, all them ingreasements in her souse-bowl, and she going empty a ladleful in the palm of your hand.

And you going raise your palm to your two lips, with your two eyes closed, to measure in intense concentration the "strength" o' this souse-prickle. You will keep your two eyes closed still, and empty the contents o' your palm into your mouth. You will start to chaw and eat, and all the time you're eating — with your two eyes still closed — you gotta say, "Hem! Ah-hem!" in testimony to the fact that the souse have a sweet fragrance o' pepper, and it blasted hot.

Water will come to your two eyes, and your throat will be cleared.

"Good Jesus Christ in heaven!" as my mother say, "*that* is souse, boy!"

Split-Pea Soup

This split-pea soup I have in mind don't have nothing to do with the thing that French Canadians famous for, something called habitant soup. I don't mean anything like broth that has a thin thin consistency, that you can see through like onion soup and them kinds o' fancy, designer soups.

My kind o' split-pea soup is the kind o' food fit for a working man. For a lighterman. A man who does pull oars in a barge, or for a man who does operate a pneumatic drill, or for a man who does shovel snow from the sidewalk when it thick and turn into ice and get hard as concrete.

This split-pea soup is *not* for a man who is a civil servant, pushing a pen all day and not sweating from his labour. As we used to say back in Barbados, this kind o' food is "man food." It will make you healthy and strong. It's the kind o' thing that does want you to lift weights, "pelt iron" and become a second Charles Atlas — all muscles.

And more than that. It does make you perform good good good in bed.

Before you start thinking that any-and-everybody can make this brand o' soup, consider the things you need to make it with, first: Split peas, of course; only the yellow split-peas would do; and these are the easiest things to cook when you are making soup. Onions, both the ordinary onions and green onions. Fresh thyme. A ham bone. Pray that somebody that you know has left back one, from a Virginia ham. If you're lucky, this ham bone going have some fat and some skin leff back 'pon it. English potatoes, meaning the kind from Prince Edward Island. *And* sweet potatoes. Don't buy Canadian yams, thinking they're sweet potatoes: you need the real sweet potatoes from the Wessindies, which don't boil away and turn to pap. Wessindian yams. Carrots. Celery. Pig tails or a piece o' salt beef. Braising beef or some other kind o' beef that have in bones. A lil cream. A lil Worcestershire sauce. Sherry (it don't matter if it is good sherry or cheap sherry or cooking sherry, any o' which will do the job just as well). Flour. Some grated nutmeg. A drop or two o' vanilla essence. And white grannilated sugar.

I forgetting anything? Well, before I finish telling you how to cook split-pea soup, I sure I going remember anything that I forget.

This food takes a long time to cook. Making it is not the same thing as opening a tin o' soup and flinging it in a saucepan to warm up, or zapping frozen food in a microwave! A lot o' peeling is involved. You got to put things in the oven and take them out, and boil-them-down in the soup. And you have to be constantly watching the pot, so that certain things don't cook too long.

But you aren't in no hurry; and basically, this is the kind o' food that doesn't take tummuch energy or thinking to prepare. So enjoy yourself whilst cooking. Relax, and pour yourself something to drink. Put on a piece o' your favourite music, like a calypso or a blues piece or some Whitney Houston. And there isn't a damn thing wrong with playing a piece o' classical music! Beethoven's Sixth Symphony.

Now you can get down to business and concentrate on the pot. If you is a working woman or a working man, and you does get nervous whilst cooking, soak the split peas overnight in cold water, and soak the pig tails in another bowl o' cold water. Before you go to work in the morning, the dust and the spoiled grains o' split peas going be floating on the top of the water. Pour them off, and put the peas back in fresh water. You may want to cover down the thing the peas soaking in. Then, lock your apartment door and go to work. The split peas and pig tails soaking safe.

Split-Pea Soup

If you know 'bout cooking and could handle yourself good in the kitchen, you know that you don't *have* to soak peas overnight. All you have to do is wash them off in cold water, two or three times, throw them in a large saucepan with cold water and start boiling them. When they come to the first boil, turn down the heat so the white stuff on the peas won't boil over and dirty up your nice stove-top; or pour off the water after this first boil, refill the saucepan with cold water and boil again. Boil and pour off.

One very important thing 'bout cooking: your cooking area, and in particular the top of the stove, have to be sparkling clean all the time whilst you cooking. You don't want people to think you is a untidy and sloppy person. Cleanliness is next to godliness, a woman tell me once.

Drop in the pig tails that have been soaking overnight, with a bay leaf, in the water with the split peas.

You going have time on your hands. So, start preparing the braising beef, or the other meat you cooking with the soup. The cheap cuts of beef, like short ribs or stewing beef or beef bones, are the best ingreasements to use.

Turn up the oven to broil. Whilst the oven at broil, wash off the braising beef with lemon and water that is cool. Dry it off with a cotton or paper towel and lay it in a Pyrex dish that you can put in the oven.

Sprinkle the beef on all-two-both sides, with a lil salt and some black pepper, and give it a thin coat o' brown sugar. Slice up some onions and throw them over the beef.

Put it in the oven now, and watch it. You not cooking

the braising beef through and through. You only want the braising beef to get brown, quick, on both sides, to keep the in-goodness inside. You only "browning" it, as we say. So, watch she good, with your two eyes like a hawk.

When one side brown, turn she over and get the next side brown too. Then, when all two sides brown, take she outta the oven and turn off the oven.

Leave the beef 'pon top o' the stove while you give the boiling split peas a little attention. If the water boiling out, add in some more. Drop the ham bone in with the peas, and don't worry your head that the bone big and look ugly.

Keep the heat at medium, and stir the peas once in a while so they won't stick to the bottom. And keep the saucepan cover-down, but not entirely cover-down. If you are a fussy person, take a ladle or a big pot spoon and skim off all that white stuff forming on top of the water.

You going start to smell the smells o' goodness when the ham bone start making a sensual thing with the split peas. Turn-down the heat a lil more lower, and cover-down the saucepan entirely.

Now turn to the braising beef. Cut it up into pieces big enough to hold in a soup-spoon and put inside your mouth. Put the pieces in the saucepan with the split peas; and scrape all the onions and the juice, those lovely ingrease-ments, from the Pyrex baking pan into the saucepan. Some of the onions going look burnt and some o' them going be golden brown. Like this, they does do wonders for the rich-ness of the soup.

Split-Pea Soup

When you've scrape-out everything from the pan, put some cold water in the same Pyrex baking pan, twirl it round and throw it in the saucepan. Soak the baking pan right away, to save elbow-grease later on.

Break off a limb o' fresh thyme, wash it off and dump the whole damn thing in the saucepan. When the soup done, you can always fish-out the stem o' thyme and fling-it-'way. Stir the saucepan so that the ingreasements won't stick to the bottom, and cover-she-back-down.

Start peeling the breadkind: the sweet potatoes, the Wessindian yams, the English potatoes and the carrots. Cut them up; and cut up some celery too. Because you are conscious o' your health, you must have all kinds o' vegetables and vittamens and iron in the things you eat. But be careful you don't put in so many vegetables and vittamens and iron that you strangle the taste o' the split peas, here!

By now, the ham bone going be disintegrated, and all the meat fall off. Take she out. Cut off the remaining meat from the bones. Cut off the skin, and throw the bone, the meat and the skin back inside the pot.

The peas should be cooked almost to a pulp, but not to a real pulp. To test them, all you got to do is mash one in a spoon. If the pea has the proper consistency, take all the split peas out o' the saucepan, put them in a dish and mash them into a real pulp. If you own a blender, you can throw the split peas in it and pulverize them.

When they mashed or blended, put them back in the saucepan with the heat still at medium or even lower.

Split-pea soup have to be thick. Thick thick thick.

The first of the breadkind to drop in the soup now is the Wessindian yam. Then the sweet potatoes. Then the English potatoes. And stir she again. If the water is low in the saucepan, full-back-up the saucepan with more cold water; or, instead o' plain water, grapefruit juice mix with water, or apple juice mix with water. Just to make style!

I just tell you a lil trick. I don't know why, but a drop or two of grapefruit juice in the water does do wonders for split-pea soup.

Now, dumpling time! A dumpling is a funny thing. There is dumplings for dryfood, dumplings for peas and rice, Jamaican dumplings, Trinidad dumplings, Guyanese dumplings, dumplings made by African Americans, and dumplings for jerk chicken. Then there is dumplings for split-pea soup — different dumplings — Barbadian dumplings. These dumplings have to be hard and thick, with no baking powder in them. Flour, water, salt, lil nutmeg and lil vanilla essence is all you need. And a strong wrist.

I use to use only white all-purpose flour to make dumplings, until a Italian woman introduce me to some flour that had in wheat bran. When I made the dumplings from this flour, man, they were stiff and nice and gluey. "Click!" my teeth cry out when I bit into one.

And a woman from Jamaica show me how to put lil cassava flour with the white all-purpose flour, mix with the wheat bran flour, in the making of dumplings. I tell you that that "click" sounded like a firecracker when I bit one!

Split-Pea Soup

If you disdain flour with wheat bran or cassava flour, add a lil corn meal flour to the all-purpose white flour when you make your dumplings.

Mix-up the all-purpose flour, cassava flour and nutmeg in the water with the vanilla essence, throw the mixture on the counter or on a board, and knead she — and knead she and knead she, till she come stiff and tight. Leave she for a while to breathe; and then you come back to she and knead she some more. It got to be stiff.

Pinch-off some of the dough and, with your two hands, roll she into a slightly elongated ball the size of a walnut, almost. Roll the rest of the dough into similar balls.

Oh Lord! Watch the pot, man. And stir. You have various meats in there, so make sure they don't stick. And watch the water level! Taste she to make sure she got in enough salt and other condiments, and that she hot enough. And whether she have-in enough thyme.

Now, bring the pot to a rapid boil. Take off the cover and, one by one, drop in the dumplings. When the last one drop-in, stir from the bottom to make sure nothing sticking. Check the water level for the last time. You going see the dumplings disappear to the bottom of the pot, and on the surface you going see lil lakes o' fat and other in-goodnesses. Now you know you in business.

Turn-down the heat to a lil above low. Add in your cream and sherry, and cover she down.

Siddown and listen to Whitney Houston, and sip the drink in your hand.

When the soup done, the water level going drop just a inch or two from the brim, and some o' the dumplings going rise to the surface. Time to serve.

Split-pea soup could be a first course or a main course. If you serving split pea as a first course, this is what you got to do. In each soup plate, ladle-out one ladle o' soup, one dumpling and one nice piece o' pig tail. Don't serve none o' the ham nor no pieces o' braising beef. In other words, don't clutter up the soup plate.

Certain guesses o' yours are sure to leave-back the pig tails without touching them. When the guesses leave, stuff the damn pig tail in your mouth and feel sorry for them!

If you serving split-pea soup as a full meal, put two dumplings, two pieces o' pig tail, two pieces o' braising beef and a piece o' each of the breadkind in each bowl or small bucket. You don't need soup plates. Put a piece o' ham skin in each serving too. Then stir the soup in the saucepan, from the bottom, and ladle-off some of this rich goodness into each soup bowl or small basin.

Do not serve the ham bone itself, nor the stem o' fresh parsley, nor the bones from the braising beef, nor the sprig o' fresh thyme. These ham bones is things that have to be left back for the cook, for members of the family or for close friends to hold in their hands, and chew and laugh as they remember the last time they taste a real ham bone or eat real split-pea soup cook with a ham bone, chew and laugh long after the respectable guesses leave.

Pepperpot

We Barbadians don't have much in the way o' hinterland nor jungle nor bush to talk about. We don't have nothing except the beaches that does wash the whole island. When it come to forests and jungles and bush, the only things Barbados can boast about, in this regard o' natural wonders, is "bush-tea." Bush-tea is a broth you could make from any bush that does grow in Barbados and that don't poison you when you drink it. If you're not careful, and if you don't know a woman with the age and wisdom of a grandmother that can stand beside you whilst you're picking the leaves and the branches of these various bushes, you might boil the wrong bush in tea and end up with either a belly-ache or slow-poisoning. Or dead.

Most o' the other islands have hinterlands and jungles and bush. And in these islands they used to have a lot o' slave rebellions. Barbadians didn't have tummuch o' these uprisings, because we didn't — and don't — have hinterlands. The only thing in the way o' black uprisings and nationalist rebellions that happen in Barbados was *one* riot, called The Riot. That was in 1938, not even during slavery. And it wasn't nothing to brag about nor write in history books. Five people get kill. Five! But hundreds get lockup. One or two fellers get deported to Jamaica, where they founded a whole new tribe o' rioters, called the Maroons!

So, as Barbadians, we're always a lil embarrass through lack o' forests and jungles and rebellions. Other Wessindians, like the Jamaicans and Guyanese, does sneer at we and say, "All-you don't have no hinterlands. All-you don't have no history. Nor no slave revolts. What the arse all-you have?"

But even though we don't have no hinterlands in Barbados, we can always lay claim to having a part in the history of the settlement o' Guyana. Back in the days when the British ruled over Barbados and Guyana (which was known as Demerara, or British Guiana), Barbadians were imported into Guyana to work as teachers, policemen, postmen, preachers and so on. These Barbadian immigrants got married to everybody they could lay their hands on and therefore helped populate most o' Guyana.

So Barbadians surely had a few hidden-away off-springs in-amongst the hunters and pork knockers of the great Guyana bush. The pork knockers were those daring men who roamed the bush looking for diamonds and silver. They got their name from the pieces o' pork they uses to eat with bread baked hard hard to last. The pork was "knocking their stomachs" — filling a hole. These was the men of the Guyana interior that Guyanese novelists Jan Carew and Wilson Harris and Fred D'Aguiar write so beautifully about, describing the mysteriousness and the frightening charm o' this deserted, dangerous area. Paule Marshall, a African-Amurcan woman with Barbadian links, went there once and wrote about how she confront the interior as a outsider, get frighten and get overcome by its wild, mysterious, compelling charm.

It is inside this bush that "pepperpot" was first conceived and cooked and eaten. Pepperpot — what a lovely name! Conjuring up all kind o' herbs and spices and meats and voodoo and witchcraft and myths.

This ancient and traditional food was first tried in the Guyana bush by Amerindians, and imitated later by the pork knockers. The pork knockers had to rely 'pon the things the land and the bush produce. They didn't take cucumber or watercress sandwiches into the thick equitorial forest; they caught and killed wild animals, to eat their flesh and suck the marrow out o' their bones.

The animals they hunted were varied, and native to the particular area where they were prospecting. Deer was on the menu, and so was labba. Labba is a polite name for nothing more than a big rat. It look like a rabbit. Perhaps the first supercilious pork knocker couldn't get a nice juicy leg o' labba down his throat till he was cajoled into thinking he was really eating rabbit. The capybara, another big rodent, weighing about fifty pounds, was desired meat, but it was probably ferocious too.

The peccaries, or wild pigs, roamed in herds. Woe betide any pork knocker who butt-up on one of these during the mating season! There was also watrass and land turtle and water dog. And iguana, or tropical lizard, which must have been a delicacy. And its blood relation in the animal kingdom, the alligator, if he did not first snap-off one o' the pork knocker's legs as a appetizer. Of course the pork knocker would have his vengeance back on the alligator, by eating-off its tail. Alligator too, as we know, is a delicacy in certain cultures.

One gets the impression that the pork knockers were catholic in their culinary taste. Nothing that walked on four legs was sacrosanct against gun and cutlass.

The bush cow, or tapir, was a thunderous prey, and could be an equally remorseless enemy. It weighs about eight hundred pounds — enough food for one whole season! But how to keep it in a fresh and edible state, especially in the sun and humidity of the jungle?

The cassava plant was the saviour. The pork knockers learned from the Amerindians that the cassava root could provide the function o' refrigeration and of curing meats.

But the pork knockers had to know their oats, for cassava does come, as any Wessindian know, in two different kinds: one is "sweet" cassava, which you does boil after you peel-off the brown skin; the other kind is "poisonous" cassava. You would grate this second kind after you skin it, and pour off the juice formed from grating it. When this juice settle at the bottom of a container, starch is formed. This starch you use to starch clothes.

The grated cassava is thinned out and put to dry in the sun. From this you make "cassareep," the essential ingreasement in pepperpot, which keeps it lasting and lasting for days without going bad, and gives pepperpot its dark colour and body.

So, the pork knocker would kill and skin a labba, and put it in a large pot to boil along with a lil salt, if available, and fresh hot peppers. When the labba cook, the cassareep was added. Then the hunter would hear a wild pig in the distance and run after it, for he didn't know how many weeks would pass before he would find silver or diamonds, and he had to stay alive. He would catch the wild pig and cut it up and add it to his pot o' pepperpot. The mixture o' various meats would cook and cook for a long time on a low heat, until the meat dark and falling off the bone.

Apart from the smoke that rose from these perpetual pepperpots, which were continually being added to with the capture of another wild animal, there must o' been a ineradicable aroma that guided the ravenous, exhausted pork knockers back to base camp after searching for diamonds

and silver all day. And this was like killing more than two
birds with a single stone o' the pepperpot pot!

Fortunately — or perhaps unfortunately — we do not have
to venture into the wilds of Guyana's bush and jungle in
order to taste this Amerindian delicacy. You could go to
Georgetown, the capital of the Co-operative Republic of
Guyana, and have it there, in any hotel or house.

Georgetown! The geographers say that Georgetown is
below sea level, but if you ever was in Georgetown, you
won't see no sea. Georgetown only have mud. If you walk
down the main street of Georgetown, a big long street,
with big trees like a guard o' honour shading you from the
sun and from the humidity (but the sun and the humidity
still pouring through on your head), you will see that the
way this street built, you would swear you was walking
down a street in Amsterdam. In the middle of the street is
this thing like an oversize trench or canal.

A lot o' places in Guyana is named after Amsterdam
and other towns and streets and places up in Holland. The
Dutch colonize Guyana years and years before the English
take over the colony. The Guyanese language is English
spoken with a heavy Dutch accent. Guyana is so much like
Holland, there is even a pair o' Guyanese boys, a Indian
and a African, who, following the example of the little
Dutch boy, have their fingers in the dyke!

A Guyanese would tell you certain lies about pepperpot and call them myths. A Guyanese woman tell me one

time, "There is a place in Georgetown, a hotel, where there's a pot o' pepperpot that's been cooking for ten years. In the same pot!"

"Do you know the name of this hotel?" I ask her. I been to Guyana a few times. Pepperpot is one o' my favourite meals. It would be easy for me to stay at the hotel with the everlasting pepperpot and taste *that* pot.

"One o' the big ones!" she tell me.

There are *two* big ones.

"The big one, man! The one where the Plantation owners does recline on the verandah in the afternoon, man!"

It could only be one of two hotels: the Park Hotel or the Tower Hotel.

Walk down that big long tree-lined street I tell you 'bout, the main drag, and *bram!* in the best spot in Georgetown is the Park Hotel. Big wide verandah. High windows like eyelids of giants. Painted green. The humidity in Georgetown bad bad. And it hot. It hot as shite. The place touching the equator. With this kind o' heat, you must need a place that have a large wide verandah to siddown in and cool-off yourself.

It is a Thursday afternoon or a Friday, after three o'clock. The banks close at three. And sitting on the hotel verandah are all these men, with a sprinkling o' Indians and Africans, but mainly white men, dress in white — white jacket, white trousers, white socks, white shoes and white Panama hats or pith helmets, with white canes if they are limping and not too erect in their posture, or if they drunk.

The only thing that isn't white is the undersides of their Panama hats or pith helmets, which are green.

This is the Guyana Plantocracy, boy! The money bags o' Guyana. The real political leaders. The holders o' futures, reputations, jobs and women. Plantation managers, Plantation overseers, Plantation bosses, Plantation owners, Plantation sons o' bitches.

I stayed at the Park Hotel, but I didn't see that mystical, continuing pot o' pepperpot. Nor did I smell the pepperpot pot.

At the Tower Hotel, I had afternoon tea, followed by drinks on the wide verandah. And nobody knew nothing 'bout no perennial pepperpot pot. But sitting there drinking water coconut with pieces of chip ice in a tall glass, you forget 'bout pepperpot and enjoy the scene.

Water coconut is better still with a generous amount of what used to be named Demerara rum in it. Guyanese, mainly politicians and artists and writers who have come out of the bush in more than one sociological sense have now named this rum Russian Bear Rum, reflecting their former political closeness to the USSR. It is one of the best rums in the world and this comes from a Barbadian who was born drinking rum!

When you see those plantocracy-men sitting down in the verandah of the Park Hotel or Tower Hotel, don't envy them their social status. You can have the same refreshment served better on the street. Stroll near the Stoebrek Market and you will see an Indian man at his cart, brandishing a cutlass in one hand and holding a green water coconut in the other. Do not run from him, giving in to your Canadian sensibilities or to your reservations as an Amurcan tourist about Indians and cutlasses and donkey carts and eating food and coconuts on the street, and think you're in harm's way. Not on this peaceable street. When the man speak, even if it sound like a scream, like a accusation, and he say, "Come! Take one!", answer his call. March right up to him, see your reflection in the gleaming blade of his cutlass, and tell him, "Gimme one, man!"

You will see, before your eyes, a display of cultural and ethnical sophistication, the clash of black hand and green coconut, the flashing silver of the cutlass, a drama you could never witness in either Toronto or Brooklyn. You will hardly see the flash of the cutlass as the Indian man cuts a water coconut to give you a drink, to cool your thirst, to conquer the humidity; a drink that the gods and the Amerindians and the pork knockers and the inhabitants of the Guyana bush have known and delighted in for centuries.

Hold your head back, raise the coconut to your two lips, open your mouth wide wide, and drain-off all. You will be carried back through time and history by the flashes of the wielding cutlass. And the pouring of the coconut water, the elixir o' the gods, will be like the mighty, rushing waters of the Kaieteur Falls.

And the real sport going now begin.

The coconut will be succulent with jelly, the colour of thick cream. Start digging-in the coconut shell, with a spoon make outta the green husk, and scrape out all the jelly. You are now in the company of the gods and spirits that inhabit the thickest jungle and bush.

I never did find that ten-year pot o' pepperpot. Perhaps it was the Emergency of 1969–70 that cause the Guyanese population, the Indians and the Africans, to be so preoccupied with killing one another that they abandoned the ten-year pepperpot pot.

At that time Guyana was a colony known as British Guiana. In the government, two ministers were involved in a power struggle: Dr. Cheddi Jagan, the chief minister, who was an Indian dentist, and Forbes Burnham, an African and a lawyer. Jagan was married to a white Amurcan woman who was a Communist. The British, fearing that Jagan's government was getting too Communist for the stability of the West Indies, suspend the constitution o' British Guiana and send in troops to keep the natives scared and obedient. Burnham resign from the Jagan government, and the racial-political lines were drawn. *Appan-jat* was born. Jagan led one party, supported by the Indians, and Burnham led the other, supported by the Africans — the People's Progressive Party, the PPP, and the People's National Congress, the PNC, respectively. Each blamed the other for the suspension of the constitution. And people start screeling, "Appan-jat!"

Appan-jat does not mean "Come for your pepperpot." It is a Guyanese word that mean what it sound like; it is an onomatopoeic word. But if you're looking for its deeper meaning, it mean "Every man for himself." Or "I going kill you, man." Or "Birds of a feather does-flock together." Indians for Indians. Africans for Africans. If I catch a Indian in my neighbourhood, woe betide that man. If a African cross my boundary, look out — one hand chop-off! The two races was divided.

Burnham later became the first president o' the Co-operative Republic of Guyana. Dr. Cheddi Jagan, after toiling and tarrying in the vineyard o' political opposition for years, and in the bush and the Guyana wilderness for donkey years, almost thirty, *bram!* became president in 1996. Burnham was dead a few years by then; he dead in office.

In 1997, Cheddi drop dead from a "heart-affection," also in office. His wife, the Amurcan intellectual, is now president. Guyanese in Guyana and Guyanese outside o' Guyana, living in Canada and England and Amurca, and in other diasporas, like the idea that his wife, Janet, is the first white woman, and the first Amurcan, to be head o' state, and president of Guyana.

So, when you talk 'bout pepperpot, a dish of great national-cultural significance, the only food that is really Guyanese, you talking about revolution, Communism, social and racial dislocation, political strife, and the Indians, Africans and British that make up the Guyanese population. Only a nice plate o' Guyanese pepperpot can bring these two factions, these fractious factions, together, make them siddown at the same political table, or the same dining table on a Sunday afternoon to eat lunch. There's no other kind o' cement that could stick these two warring factions o' Indians and Africans together.

In spite o' the myth about the everlasting stewing of pots, whether in the Park Hotel or the Tower Hotel, the point is that once you are in Georgetown you will be eating pepperpot. Anywhere in Georgetown. And the humidity of Georgetown can still kill you. So there is a very important feature that has to be present when the meal of pepperpot is being laid out on the table; this is the fan. The humidity of Guyana and Georgetown, and the humidity of Guyanese spirits, of both the supernatural and alcoholic variety, is transferred into the cultural hot-cuisine of Guyanese pepperpot. This kind o' humidity demand that you fan yourself whilst eating Guyanese pepperpot.

I was going illustrate the idea about needing a fan while eating pepperpot with a line or two from a popular calypso about fanning saga-boys or "sweet men." But it would go unheeded and unappreciated by the entire Guyanese population, both internal and those in the diasporas. Guyanese may boast of their jungles and their bush, and having the largest waterfall in the world, the Kaieteur Falls; but they can't boast o' having calypsonians of any real calibre and reputation.

The best sort o' fan is one that hangs from the ceiling, with wooden slats, and that twirls in silence. In the best public dining rooms in Georgetown there is these beautiful fans from an age of elegance, colonialism and oppression, whose breeze and fresh-blowing inducements to sleep, to doze, to nap, complete the setting for a strong rum punch before a hearty meal of pepperpot.

Needless to say, even if you eat pepperpot in a first-class hotel in Georgetown, to taste the real pepperpot you still have to ask God to help you find a woman willing and able to cook you the real McCoy, in a Guyanese home. This meal will have, in its preparation and sweet seasoning, the sweat and perspiration of cultural truth and myth. You will get from her hand the true taste of the country.

If, however, you can't get down to Georgetown or to the Guyana bush, you can still make a reasonable facsimile of pepperpot from meats you buy at any supermarket in Canada or Amurca. This pepperpot would probably be considered "bourgeoise" pepperpot by Guyanese, not the real thing that the pork knockers made to sustain strength and determination during their search for silver and diamonds in the Guyana bush. But this pepperpot is a passable version, so I suggest you try your hand at it.

Get your two hands on some beef. The best beef for this is stewing beef, or braising beef. You could even put your hands on beef ribs.

Next, get your hands on some pork — not any special expensive cut, like tenderloin. This is a meal with roots in the bush, so you have to honour those cultural and sociological antecedents. The pork you looking for is a piece o' the shoulder or the rump. And make sure it have-in bones and some skin.

Then, for flavour, you need some nice, thick pig tails. Not fresh pig tails, but the ones that salted-down in a brine barrel, that you have to stick your two hands deep down inside to get. Do the same thing with the brine barrel that contain the beef bones. Flavour is what you want: something as close as possible to that original taste experienced by the pork knockers in the bush.

Wash all these various meats in cool water with lemon juice in it, and dry them off on a cloth. Cut them up in big chunks and get out a big saucepan, one that have a cover.

Now, the seasoning. We call it "seasning," with the implication of "seize" in the pronunciation, meaning that this seasning going seize the meat in its grip, as if it have hands, and work itself right throughout the meat. So, the seasning you need is fresh thyme, whole cloves, salt (as much as you can bear), one teaspoon o' Demerara sugar, meaning brown sugar, and last but not least, cassareep. The best cassareep to use is Demerara cassareep. (Talk 'bout Guyanese being nationalistic!)

You have to boil the various meats in a pot o' water. Throw in your thyme and your salt — to taste — and your whole cloves and brown sugar.

Do not touch the cassareep yet. I will tell you when to touch the cassareep. But have it handy. And you going only need a nip-bottle o' cassareep (a bottle almost half the size of a beer bottle) for the pepperpot.

Pepperpot

Just after the meats start boiling the first time, add in half of the half-bottle o' cassareep to the water. Then, when the meats boil to your liking and to your softness, add-in the other half of the cassareep. The meats have to cook till they soft soft. Some will cook more faster than others, so watch your pot. If it mean taking out the meats that cook first, then take them out, first, nuh. And then put them back in after all the meats cook. But boil your meats till all o' them cook.

Just before you cover-down the big saucepan, drop a whole hot pepper that fresh on top o' the water. Do not cut-up the pepper. Just drop it in, whole. Cover down the pot and leave it to simmer.

Now, you have a choice o' what to eat with this pepperpot. Number one is plantains — not the ones that are ripe, that need to be fried, but green, or unripe, plantains. You would boil these, in the skin; and when they boil soft, peel off the skin and slice-them-up, at an angle. Leave them in a platter, waiting for the pepperpot.

Do not touch the pepperpot. Turn off the fire by now and leave the pepperpot to work-up some miracles with itself, letting the juices percolate through the bones and the skin. Leave the magic to happen on its own, and go back to choosing what you going eat with this pepperpot.

The second thing you could serve with it is green bananas. Now, green bananas is serious things. If you are a man cooking this pepperpot and you have a woman, do *not* give her too much green bananas. If you have to give her any, make sure, make very certain, that you give yourself two times more green bananas as you put in her plate. Green bananas have a way of making a woman incapable of stopping — and you know what I referring to! Green bananas is a "afrodizziac," suitable for men mainly. And it more cheaper and safer than Viagra. Now you know!

The third thing you could serve is hard-dough bread, close to what the pork knockers uses to eat with their jerk pork. I have to admit that the best hard-dough bread is made by Jamaicans. You can get this at any Jamaican or Wessindian store, either sliced or unsliced. If you not sure, ask any Jamaican which is the best brand out o' the two or three that you see on the shelves.

The fourth thing, and this is real nice from an ironical point of view, is "cassava hats," made from the same cassava that the Demerara cassareep is made from. Remember the grated cassava? And how you does put it in the sun to dry? Well, now you're going need it. Get a buck pot or a iron frying pan that dry and hot hot. Add a touch o' flour to hold the cassava together. Make the cassava into a ball, and then make the ball into something similar in shape to if you was making the dough for a pizza. Put it in the bottom of the buck pot or frying pan and let she get like toast, but not brown.

And the fifth thing that would go down good with your pepperpot is plain white rice. Any rice would do, but if you is a Guyanese, then you know that you have to use Demerara rice, with the long-long grains.

Now, you're *not* going use each and every one of these things — rice, plantains, green bananas and so on — to eat with the pepperpot. Just choose one or two. For example, have white rice and one or two green bananas (remembering that if you is a man, the woman must get *less* green bananas than you; otherwise you're asking for trouble!). Or have white rice and the boil plantains.

A real Guyanese would eat this with cassava hats or hard-dough bread. A Wessindian from a different island would eat it with all five choices, to make sure that it have in *all* the proper associative tastes and ingreasements.

All this time I telling you the best thing to eat with the pepperpot, you probably thinking that I forget the pepperpot itself. No. There is a reason for talking so long about the various things that go with pepperpot. The reason is to allow the pepperpot to sit. The cardinal rule 'bout pepperpot is that the more longer it remain in the pot it cook in, the sweeter it going taste. Remember the pork knockers up in the bush, going from one place to the next looking for diamonds to steal, and having to find their way back to base camp? Well, whilst they tracking through the bush and lossing their way, they didn't despair. They knew that the pepperpot pot was simmering at a low heat. And the more longer it take them to reach-back to base camp, the more sweeter the pepperpot going taste, eventually.

So, if you want to serve your girlfriend some pepperpot on a Saturday night, cook it two days before and keep it in the fridge. When you're ready to serve she, heat she up.

Pig Tails 'n Breadfruit

Whilst eating this pepperpot, pause in your delight. Close your two eyes for a moment, and into your mind will come the sparkling images o' silver and diamonds, frankincense and even myrrh and mirth, reflecting the roots of myths and culture in the bush, where some Amerindians stoop round the body of a labba or wild pig, and "oooooo-mmmed" and "aaaahhhed" while waiting for their pot to cool, all the while making you believe it was their religious devotion to transcendental meditation they was indulging in, and not that they was only expressing their anticipation of this meal, praying for the meal to finish cooking, knowing that it would have one effect upon their system when it settled in their belly: it will make them sleep, doze, perhaps dream of diamonds and silver, and more alligator tails to cut-off and boil-down in the pot that goes on cooking and cooking . . .

Pelau

Whenever I talk 'bout pelau, I have to remember my days in the fifties, at Trinity College in the University of Toronto. The food they uses to give us to eat in the dining hall was fit to take home in a doggie bag and feed to the cat. Mash potatoes that was soft and like pap. Fish cooked in a sauce that was white and that had-in lil green things. Something that look like ground beef mix-in with mash potatoes and called by the name o' Shepherd's Pie. And a lot o' vegetables over-cook and soft and served with the water drowning them — as if we was on a health kick or suffering from high blood pressure because of the amount o' studies we had to study.

We was young, strapping Wessindian young men when we arrive in Canada, and they start treating we as if we was vegetarians or convalescents. They didn't give us nothing substantial for our stomachs at all.

Then, one day in the spring, *bram!* a miracle happen. On the tables in the dining hall, something from back home appear: pelau.

Well, it wasn't *real* pelau. It was just rice cook with chicken parts in it. The kitchen staff call it pelaff. But it look like pelau, and it was close enough. It was the first and only day in two years that I left the dining hall with a full belly.

The pelau I going talk about now is the real thing. I got to give full credit to them Trinidadians, tricky as they is in matters of hot-cuisine, for perfecting this way o' cooking pelau. Especially Hettie Roach, Charlie' wife.

Trinidad's population is made up of people with many different cultural backgrounds: Africans, Indians, Chinese people from Hong Kong and Jamaica, Pottogee people from Portugal and Guyana, and others thrown in and mix up. "Outta many, one people." And outta all these various tribes comes the dish, pelau. I feel sure it is the black slaves who are mostly responsible for pelau, since yuh don't cook pelau with no curry; but I might be wrong. Pelau is cook with rice, originally grown in Trinidad by Indians. So perhaps is both a black and Indian creation. "All o' we is one!"

$\mathcal{P}_{elau}$

The Trickidadians invent it. We'll give them *that* much. But we in Barbados perfect it!

Since you can only make real pelau with chicken, it don't make sense to call it chicken pelau. With any other kind o' meat it becomes something else. But you won't need to buy a whole chicken and cut-it-up.

Pelau is slave food. It's a "make-do" kind o' food. If you have a chicken bone or a chicken back, you can "stretch" it out by cooking it in a lot o' rice. Use chicken *parts*: chicken necks, chicken wings, chicken feets, chicken backs, chicken legs and chicken gizzards. If you want to impress your friends, well, buy a whole chicken, then, nuh.

The other ingreasements you need are long-grain rice (basmati rice would do, but if you can't afford long-grain rice, buy Uncle Ben's), onions, garlic cloves, fresh thyme, dry thyme, tomatoes (or tomato paste, if you are too lazy to fork yourself down to the market, or if you are too poor to buy beefsteak tomatoes), some real hot pepper sauce (Windmill Pepper Sauce is the best), a touch o' salt, a touch o' brown sugar, and pure, simple water — although if you trying to impress somebody, like a girlfriend or a mother-in-law, you could use something which Canadians and Amurcans does call "chicken stock."

Now, here's how you would handle yourself in the kitchen when making pelau. Clean the chicken parts good, in water with lemon juice in it, and rinse them off. Dry them 'pon a kitchen towel and season them with salt, pepper, onion, fresh thyme and dried thyme.

Since I not giving you any measurements for these seasonings, you'll have to start using each ingreasement judiciously to taste. There isn't no need for me to confuse your head with measurements by telling you to use a teaspoon o' this or a milligram o' that. Instead use a pinch o' this and a pinch o' that. Yuh can't go wrong.

Leave the chicken parts with these ingreasements seasoning-them-up for an hour, or a half-hour, or maybe fifteen minutes, depending on how hungry you is. Whilst they are drawing, fix yourself a rum and soda. And put on a calypso by the Mighty Sparrow. Take yourself, in spirit, back to Trinidad for Carnival, and start dancing and wukking-up your body-line.

Now, get a big, big pot — preferably a iron pot. Put some oil in it and heat it up on the stove. When the oil hotted-up, add in some brown sugar and let it turn to liquid crystals and get more browner. Add in all the chicken parts, including the chicken feets, and stir real hard and strong, until each piece o' chicken part is covered with the oil and the sugar. Lower-down the heat right now, but continue stirring she like if you have strength in your hand.

Is time for the tomatoes (or tomato paste), so put them in, nuh, with two cloves o' garlic and some Windmill Pepper Sauce from Barbados (you could use Jamaican or Trinidadian pepper sauce instead — neither would kill you), and stir she. Cover-she-down and let she cook over a medium heat, or even a low heat if you're not in too much hurry, for about forty to forty-five minutes.

$\mathcal{P}elau$

If there isn't sufficient liquid inside the big black pot you are using, add in some water (or the chicken stock, since you're playing great!). A lil trick is to mix the water with some orange or grapefruit juice. But keep this under your hat; I don't want the whole world to know how to cook nice pelau.

After you add in the water, mix in the rice and cover she down real good. Carry on the cooking for twenty to twenty-five more minutes. When you can't see any more water in your pot, and the rice cook-in with the ingrease-ments, she done. This is pelau.

Some people does use pigeon peas in their pelau. That is up to you.

To serve she, make sure that everybody that eating have some chicken parts mix-up with the rice that you put before them. You won't need nothing to go along with pelau. Some of your greaty-greaty friends might call for a salad. Tell them to go to hell! Pelau don't need no salad. A calypso need strings and violins?

And one more thing: do not serve it piping hot. The best pelau, the pelau that does taste the sweetest, is pelau that is warm-up the next day. But if you can't wait, serve it warm, a few minutes after it finish cooking.

Pelau is one o' the sweetest foods to serve at a party or at a dance. It could feed the Five Hundred. And it does make you want to spend the whole night 'pon the dance floor, wukking up your body-line, prancing and waving, till morning come. 'Cause, the party can't done.

Oxtails with Mushrooms and Rice

inter bursting your arse. It cold. The thermostat won't get no higher than -5 degrees Celsius to give you a lil release from out o' the arms of snow and sleets. You wake up in darkness, get dress in darkness, and the road so slippery that you almost brekking a hip-bone every morning as you step outside to go to work in darkness.

The subway crowded and you still cold; and when you finish work, there you are, crawling back to your apartment over the ice and the sleets that waiting to break your arse a second time in the same day — if you slip. And you get depress. Winter still bursting your arse.

It's Friday night. You need company and something to spice up your life in this dreary place.

"What you go-do?" as the Trinidadians say. Call up a few friends? Put on the calypso, "Rahtee, Rahtee, Rah" on your stereo? Plan a lil party? Do some wukking-up to keep the blood in your body circulating?

You should. Because if you don't find something to do, you'll get more depress. Soon the ambulance going be coming straight to your apartment and tekking you away to the Madhouse, or else down to the Morgue, where they'll put you on a nice, clean white slab o' marble until your family back in the Wessindies hear and have to face the expense o' flying up to Toronto in a Bee-Wee to tek you home in a brown-painted walnut box 'pon a Air Canada plane. Oh, loss!

And when the black newspaper, *Share*, hear 'bout you and write a lil obituary, the only chorus they going sing over you is, "But I didn't know that she dead. In-true!" Or one o' your friends going say, "Wait! I rested my two eyes on that man not two days ago! Man, it was Thursday gone, when I butt-up on him in the subway. And you mean to tell me that in two-twos, in the twinkling of an eye, he *gone*? Wuh-loss!"

Yes, yuh gone. Yuh pass-away. Because it cold, and every day it dark, and you wukking all day and even with the fluorescent lights turn on, you still working in darkness. And you get depress, and yuh dead. Oh Lord!

Don't let this happen to you. Cut out this foolishness!

Try cooking some oxtail with mushrooms, serve with plain rice.

You can get oxtails almost anyplace in Toronto — in a supermarket, where they does sell them wrap in plastic, or in any Wessindian store, where you does pay through your hat for them. Wessindian merchants don't call their shops "stores" or "shops for groceries"; Wessindian merchants does call their stores "specialty shops" nowadays, girl.

But a surer and more cheaper place to buy oxtails is down in the Kensington Market. Creep out o' your apartment and brave the cold. You have to make a little sacrifice to lay out a dinner for your best friends, even if the temperature is minus 40 Celsius and your fingers and toes get frostbitten. It can't really kill yuh.

Go down Spadina Avenue where they always tearing up the road, repairing it, and where traffics always driving so fast they look like they going lick yuh down; and you swing up Baldwin Street, where you will find the European Meat Market. Go in there, but keep in mind that once you cross that threshold you going stannup for at least thirty minutes before you get serve. And remember to pull out a piece o' paper from the dispenser, with a number write-down on it.

Whilst you in there, all kinds o' people who think that they own the store going be pushing you and shoving you, while the cold wind bursting your arse every time the door open to let the next customer enter. And you pounding your boots 'pon the linoleum floor covered in sawdust, to drive warmth into your two foots and hope it travel up your two legs as you waiting and waiting for your number to be call.

But ignore that, and them. You are here on a mission, to buy two nice, big oxtails. So try to enjoy the waiting. Buy a hot dog or a cup o' coffee and listen to all the different languages that licking-down your ears. Try to pick up a word or two in Russian, Chinese or Italian. You might even get a lil advice 'bout sausages.

When they call out your number, and you manage to get to the front of the crowd and face the counter full o' meats, axe the woman to "Please give me *two* oxtails."

They does sell these nice clean oxtails whole, from the top part to the tail part. You may have to point to the exact pieces that you like, 'cause the woman serving you may not understand English too good, and you are not here in this noisy place, standing up in sawdust with all these people pushing you, to worry about speaking proper English — not even if you are a teacher in the English-as-a-Second-Language programme in the George Brown College down the street. You here for one thing: oxtails.

Try to find a way to axe the girl, who may not understand English, to please cut the oxtails at the joints for you. You may have to point your fingers at the joints, and shake and nod your head, to make she put the oxtail under the power saw at the right place.

Don't follow them Jamaicans who does cut a oxtail between the joints and then cross-cut them, giving you four pieces from one joint o' oxtail. They know more 'bout how to cook jerk pork. (I, though, have a way of cooking jerk pork — which in truth and in fact was invented in Barbados — which have some Jamaicans trying to change their citizenship and become Barbadian!)

I actually prefer the oxtails sold in a ordinary supermarket. They have a nice thick ring o' fat round the bigger pieces, and the fat is the thing that does give the oxtails flavour. But the good thing about buying the oxtails in the European Meat Market is that it is close to them Wessindian specialty shops that does sell the other things that you need, like fresh thyme, bay leaves, hot red peppers, avocado pear, limes and lemons, cucumber, fresh parsley, a head o' lettuce, mushrooms, onions, garlic, tomatoes, a small-small can o' tomato paste, bags o' brown sugar from Demerara, cloves and coconut cream. And a sugarcake or a tamarind ball to eat whilst you freezing. These are the ingreasements you going need for this meal.

The next good thing about the European Meat Market is that it's 'cross the road from a liquor store. You don't want to have to walk all over Toronto, with winter bursting your arse, just to pick up a few ingreasements. It cold, so save some steps and get home to your warm apartment, where you can drink a cup o' tea and have some Peek Frean biscuits.

At the liquor store, get a cheap bottle o' red wine for the oxtails, or some Brights sherry. After all, you're having-in friends, so put a little extra something in the food.

At last yuh get home, praise God! You have all the in-greasements for making the meal.

Now is the time to burn a stick o' incense that you buy from one of them Chinese stores near the Market. I find that the more Chinese characters the box have on, the more sweeter the incense going smell.

Light some candles. You have to create a festive at-mosphere to take your mind offa the ice and the snow and the sleets and the cold . . . *brrrrrr!* . . . and take the chill offa life. Make the most of the days which the Lord thy God giveth thee — even if your days cold as arse.

A hot calypso by the Trinidadian calypsonian Crazy filling up your place and driving the neighbours up the wall, and driving them to call the police for you. You are listening and wukking-up to "Uh coming, Uh coming," blasting down the four walls. You are in such a good mood — like a real Spiritual Baptist! Let the malicious neigh-bours get on the telephone and call the police! They could all go to hell. You not disturbing no peace; you putting life into the winter of your discontent. But on second thought, you had better be a lil cautious, 'cause Canadians don't like no noise. They carries on their life as if they are mice in a church, quiet, quiet. You had better not turn up Crazy too loud. A cold jail cell isn't much different from being laid out on a cold slab o' marble.

So, the Chinese incense burning sweet in your apart-ment, and the fresh thyme, tomatoes and cucumber soak-ing in cold water. You ready to start.

Wash off the oxtails, 'cause sometimes they does have sawdust and other things on them. Put the oxtails in a bowl with lil salt and fresh lime squeeze good. Swish them round for a minute or two, and leave them to soak for a lil while. Throw off the water, dry them off 'pon a towel and leave them on the counter.

Have a drink at this juncture. A lil red wine, preferable. But since this is Wessindian food, there isn't nothing better than a strong rum. Being a multicultural kind o' man, I myself would make a strong-strong, dry-dry martini to take the chill off my bones. Bombay Gin, no ice, and with four nice, big, green, juicy olives. I don't lift a spoon or a pot cover unless I have a drink in my hand.

And music? I can't cook a sweet potato unless Crazy or some sweet Sparrow licking-down the place with calypso.

Making food is no different from making love. Axe any woman who know anything 'bout cooking!

But this is me. You might be a Christian-minded person, and you might have solemnly vowed to don't let any kind o' spirits pass your two lips, and guard against your body moving to any music with a beat. So, drink orange juice or bottle' water.

Now, getting back to the oxtails. Put the dry-off oxtails in a big saucepan with two bay leaves.

Christ, you know something? I forget to tell you to buy a package o' beef bouillon. *Beef.* Nothing but beef bouillon. This is very important. Don't experiment with any other kind o' bouillon.

Oxtails with Mushrooms and Rice

Melt one beef bouillon in a cup o' boiling water.

Cut up two big-big onions and put them in the sauce-pan with the oxtails. Throw in some whole cloves, enough to full one teaspoon or a lil more; a lil salt; and as many hot red peppers as you or your friends could bear.

You don't want your Canadian friends to start asking for water, blowing their lips and making noise like when they're drinking hot coffee, or running too often to the bath-room while eating your oxtails. So, season them up in such a way that everybody is able to eat their belly full.

Bring the ingreasements that you just put in the sauce-pan to a boil. The minute it boil, turn down the heat. The whole apartment building is going be transform immedi-ately with the smells and aromas of your cooking.

Oxtails does take a long time to cook; and you want to cook them slow, till they get soft. Peel about six nice, juicy, fresh cloves o' garlic, and throw them in with the oxtails.

Now choose the amount o' rice you going cook. You need plain rice, or as some Barbadians call it, "white" rice.

"Boy, I cooking some white rice," a woman tell me once.

"You ever see rice that is black?" I axe her.

That was before I discover the basement of the Sin-Lawrence Market, where with my two eyes I see rice that was not only black, but brown and red too.

For this meal, though, I would cook basmati rice from India. Those Indians does grow good rice, and they know more 'bout rice than Wessindians. But you could also cook Chinese rice. The Chinese know 'bout rice too. And they know how to cook it. If you buy the rice in Chinatown, my foolish advice to you is, before you pay for the rice, make sure it isn't "sticky" rice. You need plain, perfume rice for this meal.

If you buy sticky rice by mistake, you will soon know: the rice going stick to the pot. But if you catch it before all the water boil out, add some ordinary rice, like Uncle Ben's, and the result won't be entirely like glue or Cream o' Wheat.

Put a slab o' butter in the bottom of a saucepan along with the rice, and water to suit the amount o' rice you are cooking. If you is a Wessindian or know how Wessindians does cook rice, drop a teaspoon o' coconut cream in the saucepan, and make sure that you stir she in good.

Put the rice over a medium-low heat — number 4 on the dial if you have one o' them pretty-pretty modern electric stoves. Whilst the water is getting hot, the rice grains are getting soaked, and in two-twos the rice cook, and you can count each and every grain.

Now, a few words about not serving the rice with peas of any kind. Peas-and-rice, as it is called in Barbados, or rice-and-peas, as it is known among Jamaicans, would be too much for this meal. By eating white rice, you would cut down on the richness of the oxtails cooked with mushrooms. Eating peas-and-rice with these oxtails would contradict the delicacy of the oxtails.

When the water in the oxtails boil-out and is reduced to about half the original amount, take the saucepan off the stove. Cut up another two or three big big onions, in thick slices, and add them to the saucepan. Wash off and dry the mushrooms. Either cut-up each one in two or drop them in whole with the oxtails.

Uncork the bottle o' cheap red wine and empty at least one cup in the saucepan. Empty the small-small tin o' tomato paste in the saucepan. Bring all this to a boil, stirring from the bottom to make sure that nothing is sticking. Once it boil, turn-she-down immediately, to simmer.

All your troubles end. Most o' the hard work finish. All that is leff-back to do is make the salad. But yuh know, you don't have to make no damn salad, and tired-out yourself. We Wessindians aren't salad-eating people. I don't ever remember my mother using the word "salad" when I was growing up.

"Lettuce don't have-in no goodness. To-besides! I look like a sheep to you? Or a rabbit?"

Salad, or greens as some people does call it, was something that the stocks, the animals, in Barbados used to eat. White people over at the Plantation uses to eat salad too. But if my mother's hand was twisted to make a salad to go with the main course (which she never called "the main course" but simply "the food"), she would shave a carrot.

I still hate carrots. Shaved or unshaved.

We used to grow lettuce in our kitchen garden, to put in sandwiches mostly; and I used to pretend to be a sheep and eat the lettuce straight outta the ground, sometimes without washing off the dirt. And sometimes, by accident, I would swallow a little green wirrum. But you couldn't tell the difference between lettuce out o' the ground and a fat green wirrum.

Now we living in Canada, where they say that salads are good for you. So, when in Rome . . .

I have a weakness for Romaine lettuce; and a more bigger weakness for Boston lettuce. So, wash some Boston lettuce in the sink. And since you going so far as to make a salad, why not wash some watercress, that the English like to make in sandwiches and take to the Epsoms Derby in picnic baskets?

Shake-off the water from the lettuce and the watercress hard-hard, but don't break the leaves. Since you don't possess one o' them things that does spin-round and dry lettuce leaves, you got to wrap-up the lettuce and sprigs o' watercress in paper towel, round and round and round. Leave them 'pon the counter to dry.

Get yuh salad bowl, one make-outta wood. Peel a nice clove o' garlic and, holding it in your hand, rub it all round the inside of the salad bowl. Rub and rub and rub, till the garlic rub-down to your fingernails or fingertips and nothing of the garlic leff back.

Now sprig-up the dried-off lettuce into the bowl, in pieces big enough to stick with your fork and stuff inside your mouth. Sprig-up the watercress too, and drop the pieces on top the lettuce.

Get your tomatoes. Cut them in quarters and add them to the lettuce. Sprinkle lil salt and lil white sugar.

Start stirring she up with your two hands. After you

stir-she-up, pour in lil oil and squeeze half o' lemon through your fingers. Make sure no seeds fall in the salad, otherwise they might go down somebody's windpipe and choke her, and you'll have to spend your time pounding her on her back, to prevent her from strangulating and lossing her breath and consciousness at your dinner table; and you may even have to neglect your other guesses, and take the person who swallow the seed o' lemon to the Emergency.

Get the salad fork and the salad spoon, and toss up your salad.

The very last thing to put in is the avocado pear. The avocado they sell here in Canada does get soft too quick; and soft avocado, like overripe tomatoes, does mash-up the crispness of your salad. So, wait and slice-up your avocado until just before you serving the salad.

By now, if you been taking your time, and not getting hot and sweaty like a racehorse, your oxtails will be done. They are going be soft — so soft that, if you taste one, all the meat going melt-off in your mouth. Some people like their meats soft-soft. Not me. I like to be able to bite into a piece o' meat and chew the meat between my teeth.

Only people who don't have their own teeth need oxtail to fall off the bone, so that they don't have to spend time chewing it. But you're not really suppose to suck meat. Meat is not a lollipop. Bite-in-it with your teeth, with the oil running down the two sides o' your mouth. Lick the oil from round your lips, from off your fingers. Feel the bone. Bite-in the meat again. And when all the meat gone off the bone, then, and only then, do you start sucking the bone, even if you make a lil noise. When you eat oxtail this way, you telling the person who cook the food and your host that it's damn sweet, and that you want some more.

Some people will tell you to take the oxtail off the heat to let she cool off before serving, but don't mind them. You're not going on a picnic, nor an outing. Food is to be eaten *hot*, particular in winter since Toronto so damn cold.

This kind o' food is going to taste even more sweeter heated up the next day, when all the ingreasements had a chance to work their magic into the oxtails.

To serve, all you got to do is place a little oxtail and a big oxtail on one plate. Ladle out a big heaping pot spoon o' rice and lay that beside the oxtails.

There is certainly nothing more better than piping-hot white rice. When you see all that steam rising, and you can smell the perfume of the basmati rice, and you place the first spoonful inside your mouth, Jesus Christ in heaven, you don't need nothing more better nor more healthier than this.

Stir-round in the bottom o' the saucepan with the oxtails for the thickness of the sauce, and pour a spoonful o' this goodness over the oxtails. If one of your guesses really know anything about eating this kind o' food, she going ask you to pour some more sauce over the rice too. And so asked, so do.

Don't serve the salad on the same plate as the oxtails and rice. This isn't no picnic; you don't have to pile-on everything on one plate! Keep back the salad till everybody done eating. I bet you that when you put the first plate o' oxtails and mushrooms and white rice in front o' your guesses, they going forget the damn salad.

Beer does go good with this food. If you cool, or playing cool, white wine is not bad. But if you really cool, a nice red wine will do the trick. If you are a "hard-seed," there is nothing more better with this kind o' food than a fair-sized shot o' rum in a long glass with a lot o' ice and a half-can o' soda water.

I bet anyone who eats these oxtails once will want to cook them more than once a week, from now on. But leave this meal for a Friday or Saturday night, in winter. This is special food, festive food. Food for making you feel good when you eat it.

"Man, this food is a real Afro-dizziac!" a friend o' mine tell me once.

It does make you want to do certain things in bed. If you eat this kind o' food every day as the Lord send, imagine what would happen to your body, your mind, your energy, your heart and the person you living with?

Chicken Austintatious

In Clapham Village, on Flagstaff Road, it is about three in the afternoon on a weekday, and I already home from school. I am a runner. I training. So, I run the two miles home from school.

"The athalete," my mother does call me. "Running 'bout the place like a blasted racehorse! But do you know? Nobody can't catch that boy, at all, at all! I give birth to a racehorse or a second Jesse Owens. Heh-hehaiii! The racehorse!"

I am the boy who took part, one single afternoon, in the 100-yard dash, the 220-yard dash, the 440-yard race, the

880-yard race and the long jump, on Sports Day at the Combermere School for Boys. I came first in all those events, and was Victor Ludorum. Champion of the Games. Three years later I would perform almost the same feat, on one single afternoon at Harrison College. It was thought that I was too heavy, at 175 pounds, to try the high jump to get more individual points for the championship. But at the end of this one day of track and field, I got the most points, and was Victor Ludorum, Champion of the Games.

"Like a racehorse!" my mother proclaim, when it was Harrison College's turn to see my athletic prowess. "I didn't tell yuh?"

My mother believed in my "athaletic" talent and was determined to contribute, in the best way she knew, to its development: with food. And the best food, too. Raw eggs beaten and put in Guinness Stout, with nutmeg, every morning. And steamed fish — mainly flying fish, dolphin, king-fish, shark or red snapper — every evening. She had a burning desire to keep her only son, "the athalete," champion of the games, Victor Ludorum, for life. "The racehorse."

"Boy, you hungry?"

This is the question my mother use to ask, with obvious ironical significance, since she knew how much food I did-eat already that day. She cook all our meals, including the lunch that I took to school each day. The question was her way of introducing me to the ritual, and the process built into the ritual itself, of deciding what we was going to eat that afternoon.

I liked food. I was always eating, and I was always hungry. The more food I eat, the more food I wanted to eat. I knew what my mother's food could do to me — as it did always, as she willed it to do.

The food my mother cook was never intended only "to stop a hole" in my belly. More importantly, she had it in mind that her food was to make me "feel good," make me grow into a strong young man and give me "big-big brains." Who knows whether her intention has been fulfilled?

"Boy, what the two o' we going put on the fire today to eat?" she say, with a sigh in her voice.

It is not a sigh of desperation. We have choices. They're displayed before us in the yard. We keep pigs, fowls, ducks, turkeys, sheep, and one goat for the daily supply o' milk for our green tea, chocolate tea and cocoa tea. The pig and the sheep would have to wait for the "butcher" to come. And the butcher need time to adjust his temperament to suit the disposition of the animal he was going to kill. A pig would bring him out at four o'clock on a Saturday morning, while a sheep would beckon him on a Wednesday.

Today, however, is Monday. My mother has to narrow her choices. But she still repeating the question.

"What are the two o' we going to eat this blessed evening?"

She asks this boastfully, bragging at her own undiminished circumstances.

"What about that fowl there? It stop laying eggs in the amounts I need. To-besides, I feel like having fowl. You feel like fowl?"

"Yes, Ma."

"Good!"

I anticipate the next thing she is going to say. It does not change.

"Help me then, boy! Which one to catch?"

In all these decisions about food, I function as her sous-chef, although the term had never cross her lips.

There are only two of us. My stepfather, her husband, is a policeman. He lives in barracks, and he have only two off-days a month. Without his hands, there are certain chores around the house that fall to me, that become rituals for me to perform, and engage in, and abide with.

"Help me then, boy! Which one to choose from? The grey one? The one with the red feathers? The Leghorn? No, not the Leghorn, it still laying good and often, and we getting a good price for the eggs. Not my Bardrock, neither, they more better for roasting. And I feel like having chicken boil-down in white rice this evening, don't you?"

And so said, so done.

It was easy to catch a fowl. They were kept in coops at night. They roamed about the yard during the day, and sometimes even outside the paling. You would call them "range chickens" in Canada or Amurca. To call them for feeding, my mother would shout, "Chick! Chick-here! Chick-chick-chick!" And dozens of them, in plumage of the colours of a rainbow, in all sizes and breeds, would gather obediently, cackling and squawking with excitement, very noisily at the kitchen door.

This is what happen this Monday afternoon, making it easy for me to grab one of them, the one she thinks is best for her "chicken-boiled-down-in-white-rice."

I hold the fowl in my shaking hands. She grabs it from me, by its neck. With one swing, holding the fowl in her right hand, the fowl is dead.

My mother had closed her eyes and keeps them closed. She holds her head away from the writhing, warm body of the fowl.

She puts the fowl on the ground. I watch it struggle to regain its life. My mother returns from the kitchen with the kitchen knife, a weapon with a wooden handle and a four-inch blade of sharpened steel. She sharpens the already sharp blade on the coral stone step of the kitchen.

With her eyes now closed again, she holds the fowl with one hand, and with the other slits its throat. She hates the sight of blood.

Blood mixes with the black soil in the yard, and runs over stones and white marl put there to absorb the droppings of chicken shit. The blood makes a small pool, which she immediately covers with marl and dirt.

By now, a large saucepan of water is boiling. The boiling water is poured into a basin. My mother calls any vessel that holds about a gallon of water a "basin." And into this basin of hot liquid purgatory she dumps the fowl.

It is now completely dead.

My second chore in this ritual of killing is to "pick" the fowl: pull out all the feathers as cleanly as possible. The feathers on the back and breast are easiest to pluck. The feathers under the neck and by the legs, being finer, are more difficult. I pluck the feathers with my fingers.

Lemme mention a old practice common throughout the island. To make certain that our hens that were "hard" — those that were about to lay — did not stray outside the backyard and lay their eggs on a neighbour's property, and to make sure that the hens were ready to lay eggs on that day, we had to "feel" the hens. To feel a hen, you hold the cackling, struggling hen upside down with one hand, and push the little finger of the other hand inside the fowl's pooch to search for a hardness that suggests an egg.

In Barbados, which is a real litigious place, with quarrelling and fighting and lawyers and policemen, women are always tekking their neighbours to court. You can see them every day, Monday, Tuesday, Wednesday, Thursday and Friday, standing in the Court Yard under the berry trees, whose pods fall on their heads. The owners of hens are laying charges. Their hens have laid their eggs in the backyards or under the cellars of neighbours, and the neighbours have claimed the eggs as their own!

When I have pick the bird, accumulating in the process a red moustache and a goatee from the flying feathers, and with my arms hairy as those of giants I was reading about in adventure books, my mother draws a line with the knife across the breast of the fowl, leaving a widening mark of red on the black dirt of the yard. Out tumble the guts, liver, heart and unhatched eggs.

On these occasions, with the sight of all this blood, my ambition to become a doctor (which was really my mother's ambition for me) vanished. My mother digs a hole in the ground and buries the guts. The liver, the heart and the unhatched eggs are good for you, make you strong. We eat them.

She dumps the fowl into a large Pyrex bowl that contains salt and fresh lime juice. Her butchering begins.

Since everything, every part of the fowl, is going be eaten, and as it is only my mother and me to eat this whole fowl, she places no preference to the way she chops up the fowl. Breast is not separated from back, nor breast from wing, nor thigh from leg. She chop-off the toes of the fowl with the nails; the rest of the chicken feets we are going to eat. The head is saved too, for eating. And the unhatched eggs provide a delicious snack, resembling caviar in its preciousness, when she drop them in a light batter, with hot-hot fresh pepper, into hot lard oil. "Caviars!" she say.

So, we have the head, the neck, the tips of the wings, the breast and the back, all cut up in pieces to suit my mother's impulse. The parts she place back in the Pyrex bowl, to draw, after she wash them four times thoroughly in salt and lime juice.

Then the pieces are dried with a cloth and put back into the Pyrex bowl. Fresh thyme, fresh ginger, salt and slices o' fresh green onions, onions and fresh hot peppers are now mix in them, using your two hands.

My mother believe in "feeling-up" her meats. She does use her fingers to mix in the ingreasements, or what she calls the "in-goodness."

"We cooking fowl boil-down-in-white-rice," she says more than one time. I hear her voice from the other room. She has this habit o' talking to herself, out loud, what she is about to do. Whether it is washing clothes, giving me a flogging or putting on her clothes, she goes through verbally all the stages of each act, as if she is trying hard not to forget.

"The Demerara long-grain rice already pick. I pick it this morning after you went-school. And I pass it through water two times, washing it. Lemme put some water in this pot for the rice, now. Now I going-bring the water up to a certain level, yes . . . about here is enough, 'cause you don't want the water in the pot with the rice to be tummuch, to make the rice soggy and stick. Soggy rice is the worst thing you could have, if you eating it with boil-chicken, seeing as how the fowl have-in its own juice and will spring water."

She uses "chicken" and "fowl" as if they is one word.

"Lemme take out a little o' this water. Now, a pinch o' salt. That would do. Lil salt meat . . . I have any salt beef? Or pig tail leave-back from the last time? I have salt beef, man! Salt beef going-go better with the boil-chicken. Wash it off good, so that it won't have-in tummuch salt, to make the rice too salty. A little sprig o' thyme from offa my tree, and cover-she-down . . . and that's that! Boy, we cooking!"

I look at her and wonder. This woman is a poet.

"Whilst I busy finishing-off the fowl, I want you to watch the water to see when she boil, hear? Don't let she boil over. Call me the minute you think she going boil over. Hear me?"

My main function as my mother's sous-chef is to "watch the pot." To watch the pot is to see that the water does not boil over, or that the pork chops are not burning, or that the water does not boil out of the rice.

When the chicken and rice are cook, my mother and I will eat-off all this sweet food, the whole chicken. Chewing the feet, relishing the skin and the head, which my mother say "contains the supstance for making your brains more bigger, boy! In order for you to read the Latin books you have to learn at Cawmere School for Boys. Understann? Good!"

She says this as she cracks a bone from the leg and sucks out its marrow, in a noisy slurrrrp.

When we finish, and the bones are tossed into the yard — on the marl and the dirt hiding the blood of the fowl — for the dog, Rover, to crack even finer, I wander through the neighbourhood, chewing the eyeballs of the chicken, pretending they are two gobs of Wrigley's chewing gum in my mouth.

My reservation nowadays 'bout cooking chicken and eating chicken is really base on the enormous amount I uses-to eat whilst growing up in Barbados, in Flagstaff Road. I eat it fried, boil, roast, bake, boil-and-then-fried, fried-and-then-boil-down, and in a form my mother call "friggazee."

And in Toronto, years afterwards, I eat chicken after chicken, cooked in various strange North Amurcan ways. During my years as a student at Trinity College, I devour a lot o' chicken at the Swiss Chalet on Bloor Street near Bedford, near the college. This version o' cooking chicken was strange to me. It had a new and fascinating taste o' something call a barbecue. I never taste barbecue-chicken before I land here. But I soon grew out o' that liking for Swiss Chalet chicken.

When I was-teaching at Duke University in Dur'm, North Carolina, a black fellow, a graduate student, introduce me to Southern fried chicken. Southern fried chicken in Dur'm is the best in the world! I use to buy it at Chicken Box Number One or Number Two. Needless to say, if you fortunate enough to have it cooked by a Southern family and not in a restaurant, you getting the very best.

I have a friend up here, John Henry Jackson, who born in the South, the first black man to quarterback the Toronto Argonauts. When John Henry-J make a fry-chicken for you, Jesus Christ! John-Henry's chicken does considerably outstrip *any* that Swiss Chalet, Kentucky Fry or the two Chicken Boxes make, including all the other versions o' fry-chicken that the various fast-food places in North Amurca does-make.

Nowadays, the only way I does cook chicken is a dish that I make, and mainly for friends, call African Chicken. A student, Orde Coombes, teach me how to make it when I was a professor at Yale University in 1968. He was one o' those black-Amurcans (hyphenated in them days) who was rediscovering Africa, a political strategy to combat the degradation and segregation he and others was experiencing through the slow pace o' "racial integration." He dead now, pass away; but I don't think he mind if my recollection of his African chicken recipe is not exactly perfect.

If I only master it partially and remember half o' what he show me, and if its smell is the same delicious anticipation o' cultural lasciviousness as his-own, then this African chicken shall rise up among the clouds and create a musical riff in the strains Orde Coombes must be playing in his retirement, while cooling-out on a soft cloud.

If you want to make this dish, you need a chicken.

The size o' the chicken should suit the number of mouths you have to feed. Personally, I would not get a whole chicken but chicken parts: the legs, the neck, the wings, the thighs and the back. If your preference is the leg with a bit of thigh attached, you could buy and cook as many o' these pieces as you like. With a whole chicken, you have only two legs and two thighs! (Unless you happen to be living in Barbados in the days during the war, when some people who raise chickens claim that they had chicks that was hatch walking on *three* legs each!)

You need a few other things as well, base upon the amount o' chicken parts you going cook: an onion, green onions, fresh thyme, cloves o' garlic, fresh ginger, brown sugar, pepper, fresh red peppers, cream, mayonnaise and peanut butter. The peanut butter should be the one that don't have chunks in it, but if you only have the chunky one, don't panic. Since you going be putting the peanut butter in a blender, the chunks going get beat up to a pulp.

Wash-off the chicken parts and place them in a bowl with a lil salt and lime juice, or lemon juice. While they soaking, chop-up the onion, dice the green onion, and either slice the cloves o' garlic or press them.

When you have all this done, dry-off the chicken parts on a towel, and using your ten fingers, rub-in the chop onions, the green onions, the fresh thyme and the garlic thoroughly into the flesh o' the chicken parts. Throw a dash of salt and a few flings o' pepper, to suit your tolerance, on all sides o' the chicken pieces, and sprinkle them lightly with brown sugar. Rub the brown sugar into the chicken with your two hands. Then pour a lil vegetable oil, or butter, or even drippings, over the pieces, and place them in a large baking pan.

At this point, turn the oven to broil; and after a few minutes — perhaps ten, or when you can see the element turn red — put the uncovered pan o' chicken in the oven.

All you want to do at this stage is to brown the chicken on both sides to seal all the in-goodness inside. You are not cooking the chicken.

There is a thing about chicken. If you boil it in the peanut-butter sauce without putting it under the broiler first, the colour of the chicken when done is going be a little like unhealthy skin. It might have a delicious flavour, but aesthetically it going look plain. Food does taste better and sweeter when you present it with a lot o' colours.

As you reading this, keep one eye on the oven to make sure that the chicken is browning nice without being cooked. When one side is brown, turn the pieces over to get the other side brown too.

And you remember something that you did not buy now, because I forget to tell you, but that you need to go with this meal: sherry. You would say that white wine is natural and suitable for chicken, but I suggest that for making peanut-butter sauce, a deep, sweet sherry or, if you can afford it, brandy or red wine is better. I does use sherry, or brandy when I have it, because the sherry does give a deeper, more burnt flavour.

All this time, keep a eye on the chicken in the oven. And if you are the kind of person who can do two or three things at the same time, wash the dust from your blender and dry it.

Wait until you take the chicken parts, that is now brown, out of the oven before you start to work on the peanut-butter sauce. You won't need the oven again.

Put in the blender two or three heaping tablespoons o' peanut butter; one green onion, sliced; one tablespoon o' mayonnaise; and some fresh parsley, if you have it, to raise the colour of this concoction of ingreasements.

Add the hard liquor — sherry or brandy — of your choice. Whichever you use, you need only as much as you can take. When I use sherry, I does pour in two jiggers. If you using wine, I suggest you pour-in a generous amount — but not more than half o' cup.

Cover the blender tight, switch it on, and go to town blending these ingreasements. But suppose you don't have a blender? Use an egg-beater or lick-up the mixture with a fork.

When these ingreasements blended, add in a half of a quarter cup of cream.

I have a lifelong aversion to milk and cream and custards, and things that when cooked, retain any trace o' those colours. White and cream remind me of hospitals, and of being forced to eat or drink medicinal things. I refuse to eat anything anybody tell me is "good" for me. This is why I suggest you add green onions in the blender, to give a more lifelike colour to the peanut-butter sauce.

If you are like me and happen to have a few leaves o' spinach hide-'way in your refrigerator, break them up and add them to the blender as well.

When the peanut-butter sauce is properly blended, you are ready for the final stage. Put the chicken parts from the baking pan into a very large saucepan. Put it on the stove and bring the chicken to a slow boil. If you do not have the chicken at a slow boil, there is a chance that, when you add the peanut-butter sauce, the chicken parts going dive to the bottom o' the pot; and when you hear the shout, "The damn thing burn-up, man!" You don't want that.

So, before you add the contents of the blender, bring the chicken parts to a slow boil. When they are boiling, pour the peanut-butter sauce, *slowly and evenly*, all over the chicken, and immediately turn down the heat. Stir the contents thoroughly, from the bottom, and let them simmer.

Is at this stage, if the colour in the saucepan is too whitey-whitey or creamy-creamy, that you could cut up another green onion, or a few leaves of fresh parsley or spinach, and add them to the pot, to add a healthier colour to your food.

The chicken must be cooked slowly. You don't want to use a rapid fire and end up with a saucepan o' skin and bones, with all the chicken meat drop off, as if you are making soup.

Now, add some fresh hot peppers — not a handful, but a few slivers snip-off with a knife or a scissors. You can also add some slices o' sweet pepper. Red peppers add a wonderful contrasting colour.

Cover the saucepan, and pray to God.

Now, what to eat with this chicken? You may serve anything with it, but as you know, there is one thing that goes with chicken best: rice. So, as we say in Barbados, cook "some steamed white rice." Use good ole Uncle Ben's, or a nice long-grain rice. The rice should be cooked so that the grains are soft, but you should still be able to count each and every grain.

Or you could get some nice English potatoes. Peel and wash them, and slice each one in four, lengthwise. Put them in boiling water, and just before they are almost completely cooked, take them out and pour cold water over them to arrest the cooking. In other words, you just scalding them.

Put them in a large baking pan, with a generous amount of olive oil, and put them in the oven. Bake them to a golden brown, and to a crispiness that no hamburger joint could match.

Or you could buy some Wessindian sweet potatoes and boil them in their skins (as every vegetable should be). When they cook, use a sharp knife to lift-off the skin. Shake the potatoes around and around with some parsley flakes, some cloves o' garlic and a little olive oil or butter; and put them in a baking pan in the oven for a few minutes.

Do you want a salad too? Probably because you aren't a Wessindian. OK, but the salad you make *must* complement all the tastes of the chicken cooked in peanut butter. It should have a opposite tanginess. The onions that you put on the chicken going be burnt dark brown from being under the broiler, and this will give the chicken a smoked flavour. So, complement this taste with a salad of fresh spinach leaves, Romaine lettuce and spring tomatoes cut in halves, and tossed; and use a dressing of sugar, salt, white pepper, lemon juice and a dash or two of olive oil. Just before you serve the salad, add a dash of Worcestershire sauce.

Whilst waiting for the salad to come together, add one or two or three dashes o' Worcestershire sauce to the chicken parts in the saucepan. Stir for the final time, and serve.

The first time that I cook African Chicken, a friend, in her enthusiasm, and after eating-off most, christen the dish Chicken Austintacious. I am happy with that name. I think Orde Coombes up in heaven happy too.

Omelette
(made with sardines)

We was looking for either Chicken Box Number One or Chicken Box Number Two. And we couldn't find neither one, at all, at all. It was after ten o'clock one night in summer, and it was dark. And we was in North Car'lina, y'all!

And we was hungry.

And thirsty.

And I couldn't drive too good. I had just bought a second-hand Mercedes-Benz from up in Chapel Hill the week before, and to make matters worse driving-wise, it had a standard-shift gearbox.

A black feller ask we, "What's happ'nin, bro'?"

And we tell him, "We looking for the Box."

"Yeah?" he say. "The one where you nearest, *close,* brother. Close like a motherfucker. But the one in the 'Hood still open . . . *Maybe* it still be open. Try the one in the 'Hood."

We was looking for a liquor store too.

"But Dur'm dry, brother," the feller tell we. "Dur'm be a dry town. Dry as a motherfucker!"

Vroom-vroom! Bram-bram! Brax-brax! I licking up the gearbox, and then I drive-off in third, instead o' first gear. But we gone-'long down some dark roads in Dur'm, me and my friend, Norman. Norman Mailer and me. And in the motor car with we is Norman's bodyguard, who have a black belt in karate!

We was, the three o' we, hungry-hungry. When I tell you hungry? If you haven't been hungry in a Southern town, you haven't been hungry in your life. Particular on a night when it dark and all you can smell is the magnolia trees!

I didn't know Dur'm too good. I had left Canada to teach at Yale, then at Brandeis, then at Williams College in Massachusetts. Then I was offered a position teaching Black Studies at Duke University. It was as if I was being led ever farther south, back to Barbados where I was born.

It was 1972, and I was embracing the black Amurcans and black Amurcan culture: Leroy Jones, Larry Neales, Paule Marshall, Miles Davis, John Coltrane and them-so. Everything those days was "black cultural nationalism";

and I was ready for it. I was even trying to speak like a black Amurcan.

The chairman of the black studies programme at Duke drove we down from New York to teach at Duke in his old, rattling, beat-up Thunderbird, which had to get fix — water pump, air-conditioner, brake fluid — every time we stop for gas. He was from the South. I met him at Yale, where he was a gradual student in religious studies and where he take one of my courses in African Amurcan literature.

We had just stop at a place in Baltimore when he say to me, "We just pass the Mason-Dixie line, brother!"

I looked nervous out the window, hardly able to see the road for the dust on the glass, wondering what I do to myself by accepting this one-year appointment at Duke.

"The Mason-Dixie?" I ask him, still looking to locate a line, a boundary, a sign, something to indicate and express the apprehension I start feeling on my first journey into this turbulent part o' the country.

"You can't see it," he explain. "It's just a imaginary line, bro'. I know when I pass it . . ."

Living in Dur'm and teaching at Duke, it was easy for me to pretend that I was a black Amurcan, and wallow in pecan pie, Virginia ham and, above all, Southern fried chicken.

I was introduce to the Chicken Boxes: "It be the best goddamn chicken this side o' the Mason-Dixie line, brother!" Chicken Box Number One was in the "white district" that surround the Duke University campus. Chicken

Box Number Two was in the "black district," where black North Car'linians had barber-shops, bookstores that sold the Muslim newspaper, and drugstores stocking cosmetics for black skins and pomades for black hair; where Aretha Franklin screamed from loudspeakers that erupted onto the wide sidewalks; and where I was lulled into this new, black, cultural, determinist nationalism. I considered myself to be as much a Southerner as a Barbadian.

So when Norman Mailer arrived to give a lecture at the University o' North Carolina up in Chapel Hill, and a lecture at Duke University, I did-know I was going introduce him to the cultural-culinary delicacies o' the South. I *know* that Norman was going get his first real taste of the South by eating chicken in one of the Chicken Boxes.

I felt no hesitation; no scepticism about his appreciating chicken cook by Southern black hands; no suspicion that he going find any o' this strange and outside *his* Brooklyn cultural references. No. 'Cause after all, he already had-write *White Negro* in which he put himself into a ring against James Baldwin; and when I meet him the first time at Yale University, he had just publish a long, incisively critical piece on the state o' "the Negro problem" in *Look* magazine.

When we fail to locate Chicken Box Number Two, I decide that my reputation is at stake, that I cannot allow my ignorance about social life in Dur'm to confound my responsibilities to a friend. You can't have a famous author in a Southern town with no chicken-places open, and have him spread the news back up North about we Southerners!

So, I get a brainwave. I remember a professor with the same name as me, Clarke, who had to be living somewhere in Dur'm, 'cause Dur'm small. And I know that Professor Clarke holds my friend Norman in high regard. As God would have it, I find Professor Clarke name in the university directory. And I call-he-up. As it happens, Professor Clarke is doing a gradual students' seminar the very next morning on the religious and moral determinants in Norman's *Armies of the Night*. And Professor Clarke, being chairman of religions at Duke and a Christian-minded, Christian man, tell we, "Come! This is great! Come!" He tell we that he going call some faculties and some gradual students. And regarding the libations and the need for such, there is no need to worry, and no lack, thereof, of those beverages.

So then, *vroom-vroom-vroom! blam-blam! brax-brax!* I get the second-hand motorcar in the right gear for driving off. Professor Clarke's invitation is like oil greasing the gearbox of the second-hand standard-shift Mercedes-Benz. Me and Norman, and Norman's black-belt bodyguard, drive through Duke Forest, where the senior faculties does live in big houses, and although we make three wrong turns and have to turn back four times, and then take two more wrong turns, we finally arrive in front o' Professor Clarke's mansion, more hungry and more peckish than before — two hours later — for a drink. It is eleven-something, now. Late to be visiting somebody in the South.

"It's an honour," Professor Clarke say, meaning Norman. "Charmed," he say, meaning the woman with the black belt in karate, who was young and pretty-pretty. "How are you, Professor?" he say, meaning me.

And all o' we start to apologize, and tell Professor Clarke what a nice man and a nice Christian he is; and how we make six wrong turns and had to turn back five times; and how it dark in Dur'm when the magnolia trees start to bloom; and how they isn't no street lights in Dur'm, like up North and how the town dry as a bone and, as the black feller in the 'Hood say, "Dry as a motherfucker!" — although we didn't use them words in the hearing of a professor who teaches religions and who live in a forest, Duke Forest — and how the Chicken Boxes of Dur'm and North Car'lina, Numbers One and Two, is always shut when a man is hungry and a man can't get a chicken bone to suck on or eat.

We're stannin' up in the kitchen, which is big, and Professor Clarke say, "Help yourself."

"Help yourself, Professor," he say a second time, while Norman is telling the members of the faculties and the gradual students about *Armies of the Night,* and about the moral imperatives and the socio-agricultural properties in the book.

When I open the door o' the fridge, big as a three-storey apartment building, Jesus Christ, the amount o' food! Turkeys, roasts, chickens, beef steaks, chicken parts, turkey parts, eggs, sausages. My God in heaven, the poultries and the carnivories and the fish!

Omelette

And I try to see if Professor Clarke, who I don't think come from the 'Hood, is cool. I look to see if his larders and shelves, high as the insurance building in downtown Dur'm — the tallest building in the state, own by a black man, too — contain certain ingreasements. And after I find the hog maws and the chitlings and the corn bread and the hominy — hominy grits in this mansion of a holy man — I know that Professor Clarke is "cool as a motherfucker!" as the black feller would say.

While Norman gone to town on a question from a member of the faculties — "In your opinion, Mr. Mailer, and considering the socio-political primary aspects of your dissertation, namely in *Armies of the Night,* do you think it is reasonable to posit, as I am prepared to make the position, because the point I am trying to make . . ." — I try a Scotch and soda, with more Scotch than soda, and take out some eggs, cream, butter, green onions, thyme, parsley flakes, garlic powder, salt and white pepper. And three tins o' sardines. I eat the first two tins o' sardines by myself, 'cause I was still hungry. And I save-back one, to put in the omelette that I was going to make for Norman and the karate-woman, and for me.

I find a frying pan that was made out o' iron, and that was two feet in diameter and yellow on the outside. There is such pretty things in the South! Like the smell o' magnolia trees on a dark night.

I wash out the pan and put half a block of butter in it, to warm up the pan and get acquainted with it.

And then I turn off the heat.

In a big bowl, I break up all twelve eggs, and I cut up the ingreasements in the same bowl: onions, not too much; green onions, not too much; parsley flakes, not too much; garlic powder, not too much; and some oregano I find, not too much; and some basil I find, not too much. And using a fork, I mix up these ingreasements with the twelve eggs. I do not tamper with egg-beaters, nor nothing that is mechanical!

Now I mash-up the tin o' sardines with a fork, along with the oil or juice in the tin, and empty it into the eggs. And I stir and stir, and beat and beat, until the ingreasements in the bowl was smooth smooth smooth, in a nice paste-like consistency. And I pour in a lil cream, just to make the ingreasements more smoother and even.

For the hell of it, and to make up for time loss in tracking-down the Chicken Boxes, and also to fit into the greater wealth and ambience of the senior faculties, most o' whom live in these woods, I went in the liquor cabinet and choose the most expensive sherry that my namesake have; and I uncork she; and I pour a good shot in a sherry glass; and I raise my head and hold back my mouth, and empty the contents thereof into my mouth — just to try it, and to make sure I was using the best sherry. And then I pour some sherry into the eggs.

If Professor Clarke didn't have sherry, I wouldda use rum; and if not rum, Scotch; and if not Scotch, Wild Turkey Bourbon; and if not bourbon, wine; and if he didn't stock white wine, red wouldda do. If we wasn't in Duke Forest where the senior faculties live, and if we was back in the 'Hood, I wouldda use anything — even beer.

Warm the frying pan now. Hold the frying-pan handle in your hand and make the butter that melt move evenly over the whole bottom o' the pan. But don't let it get too hot. You could, if you wasn't drinking Wild Turkey or Ballantine Scotch or anything, raise the frying pan to your face to test the heat. This is the best way to test the heat of a frying pan that you going cook omelettes in! The only way.

Make one omelette at a time, regardless o' how many mouths you have to feed. Pour-in some batter, and let it spread at ease and with freedom all over the pan. As you gaze on this rich concoction, you will see the edges of the omelette start to cook first. Watch for that. Then get a spatula in one hand and a spatula in the next hand, and move them — easy, easy, now! — underneath the omelette to make sure she not sticking to the pan.

When a lil more of the edge cook, it's time to turn she over. Turning over a omelette is a art. You don't turn over a omelette the same way you turn over a pancake, or a bake, or a piece o' liver. With a omelette, you dealing with nuances, with implications, with innuendo. You have to fall in love with the omelette first, before you can touch she. And when you touch she, remember that you touching something precious and fragile, like the body of a woman you love.

It is all touch.

So, when you turn over the omelette, turn she over only one-third o' the circumference. And turn the opposite side only one-third over too. Then, and only then, should you dare turn over the whole omelette.

Norman and the bodyguard move into the omelettes as if they was Southern fried chicken; and some o' the gradual students and some o' the faculties, caught up in talk 'bout the dialectics o' showing that *Armies of the Night* is really a religious tract, or a moral tract that touch the nerve of Amurca, a crisis o' morality that the whole country was going through at this time, stop arguing and start greasing. And I watch the whole four or five batches o' omelettes disappear.

The morning sun was seeping through the trees before the platters o' omelettes was replenish. And when we left the home of the good professor, it was six o'clock, and he was early for his nine o'clock seminar with his gradual students in Ethical Religions. Norman and me and the lady with the black belt drive slow slow slow out from Duke Forest. The old, bottle-green, second-hand Mercedes-Benz was driving like a new car. And as we drive 'long a long road with tall trees on all two sides o' the road, I see a feller and honk my horn at him to tell him, "Be cool, brother!" He do something with his mouth and his lips, and I imagine that the word that leave his mouth is "Motherfuckers!" but we don't care, neither me nor Norman nor the bodyguard. And

Omelette

we don't give a good goddamn about nothing nor nobody, 'cause we isn't hungry, nor dry, nor feeling peckish, nor care that Dur'm, North Car'lina, is "dry as a motherfucker!"

We was cool, man!

Drinking Food

You does hear a lot o' stories, mostly myths, about drinking; a lot o' 'nancy stories 'bout fellers who does drink all day and all night, and still don't get drunk because they don't mix their drinks.

"I does drink my drinks *straight*, man!"

"I don't take nothing sweet in my liquor, man!"

"Drink water? Or anything so? In my drink? This liquor too pure to spoil the taste and the body with water, man!"

"The easiest way to get drunk is for a man to mix his rum with Coke or ginger ale or anything so."

"If you chasing your rum or your whiskey with *anything*, chase it with *water*. Well, even soda water, then."

If you share these opinions o' drinking as a man or a woman (and there are women in Barbados that can — and do! — drink *any* man under the table), before you start drinking, you still need something on which the liquor must rest.

"We don't drink liquor on a empty stomach, man! You think we stupid?"

You need a lil "drinking food." This is food to form a base, or layer, with which to absorb the liquor. As my mother tell me once, years ago, "If you know that you going be drinking a lot o' liquor in the evening, you make-sure that you line your stomach with some good food, hear! Nothing beats a nice, mellow bowl o' cou-cou and salt fish."

I wonder how she know.

The origins o' drinking food lie in the rum shop, which is a café or small bar where you will always find a bottle o' water, a bucket o' "chip-ice" and a full bottle o' rum on the counter.

The water is usually kept in a large bottle that once contained rum, either in a small fridge (which was rare in the forties) or on a large block of ice. Generous amounts o' sawdust poured on the block o' ice does make the ice melt more slower in the heat. The chip-ice was cut from this block with a ice-pick. Many rum-shop keepers perform this daring feat by driving the ice-pick through the block o' ice whilst holding the ice in their palm; and never, in my

time, have I ever see a dot o' blood spurt from a shopkeeper
hand as a result o' chipping ice.

When you go in the rum shop, you pour your rum in a
shot glass and you fires it back in your mouth, in one fling.
You squeezes up your two eyes, shut tight, against the sting
o' the rum, and you say, "Hem! Ah-hem!" This is to make
the rum-shop owner know that he selling real good strong
rum; and also to impress your drinking buddies with your
understanding of the full protocols o' drinking rum in a
rum shop; and to clear your throat. And then, and only
then, you pours a lil water in the same shot glass, to wash
down the rum. Finally, you have to say, "Ahhhh!" And you
says it with gratification.

This is real, true-true rum drinking.

And before you get more further into this ritual, the
rum-shop owner going serve you a lil something that he
prepare for you to eat whilst you drinking the rum: dry and
crispy biscuits. These biscuits may be imported or made in
Barbados. They is a favourite drinking food. When the rum-
shop owner serve you these biscuits, a statement concerning his class, and the class o' the rum shop, and the amount
of business he does be doing selling rum, is being made.

The biscuits does be serve with cheese, sometimes. But
if you is a person of class, the rum-shop owner going serve
the biscuits with corn beef.

Although the food you eat while you are "firing your
darrou" — drinking your snaps o' rum — is really the re-
sponsibility of the owner of the rum shop, and although the

shopkeeper does provide it to his customers without charge, I'll tell you how to prepare corn beef as a drinking food.

To begin with, the corn beef has to be Fray Bentos, from the Argenteen. Nothing less, in the way of manufacture, will do. After all, this food is going into your stomach, and you should always put the best you can afford in your stomach.

Cut up a lot o' onions and put them in a frying pan that have in oil. Ham skin will do, or drippings from the bacon or roast pork you had on Sunday. For style, add some sweet peppers. Red is a pretty colour, but there ain't nothing wrong with green sweet peppers. Stir-round these ingreasements in the frying pan. Add-in a lil fresh hot pepper, or sprinkle some black pepper over she.

When these ingreasements are sawtaying, empty the corn beef into the frying pan, and stir. The minute the corn beef change colour, it done.

You don't necessarily have to fry the corn beef. Sometimes, depending upon the time o' day and the amount of time the men and the shopkeeper have on their hands, corn beef is served straight from the tin, with pieces of fresh hot pepper, thick slices of onion and a generous dousing of hot pepper from a bottle, mixed in.

The main thing about drinking food is that it should contain a *lot* o' hot pepper. A drinking man does argue that the hotness of the food is what keeps you sober. But I don't suggest you try out this philosophy: you'll get blind drunk, and your mouth will be on fire!

Men drinking rum in a rum shop does hold out their hand and receive a lil corn beef in it, and after they devour this, hold out their hand again and receive a drop o' pepper sauce in it. The sound they make after eating the hot sauce is similar in its onomatopoeic significance to the sound made when the first mouthful o' dark rum hit the palate: "Ah-hemmm!" It declares that the rum and the corn beef meet the high standards nourished in this particular rum shop.

Another kind o' drinking food is salt fish. You can eat salt fish raw: just put it in your mouth and tear-off a piece. Since it is drinking food, you don't want to waste too much time preparing it, but you could boil it.

Put the salt fish in a saucepan with lots of water. Bring it to a boil. Throw the water off, full-back-up the saucepan with fresh water and bring it to a boil again. This can be repeated four times, until the fish is cooked. And the excess salt, boil' out.

The white outer skin is clean-off and the bones taken out. Sprig-up the salt fish into lil pieces. Put some onions, green onions, fresh sweet peppers and red-hot, mouth-scorching fresh peppers in a saucepan, and let them sawtay; and then, on top o' this, throw the pieces o' salt fish, and stir.

Fish cakes made from salt cod are also served as drinking food. Nowadays, however, cod fish from Newfoundland is very expensive in Barbados, so fish cakes are not free any more; you got to buy them.

Drinking Food

The best night for eating drinking food is a Saturday night. The rum-shop owner and his wife have kill a pig the Saturday morning. The shopkeeper, if he is in a good mood, would share his bounty with his friends and best customers, and serve some pork chops, or harslick, or pudding and souse. This would be served in the back room.

The rum shop was always operated on the basis of class distinctions. At the bar in public view, anyone could fire his darrou. But men such as the schoolmaster, the postman, the policeman, the chauffeur of the large black Humber Hawk belonging to the owner of the Plantation or to the Commissioner of Police, the barrister-at-law who visited his "out-side woman" in the village — these village dignitaries were invited to take their seats in the back room.

In the back room there were better chairs, an oilskin cloth on the table, and sawdust on the floor, which was swept two times a day. The chip-ice was more plentiful, the drinks were poured with a "lil touch for goodwill," and the possibility of fish cakes — "on the house, man! Jesus Christ, man! I not going go broke from serving you a few fish cakes, man! Goodwill, man!" — was greater. But only the special customers would know of this beneficence.

Never once, in all the time I been watching these proceedings in the rum shop, and later, when I come to take my place in the back room, did I ever see a woman stand at the bar of the rum shop to take her waters.

And with these rituals and customs and myths go a kind o' cultural attitude and style to drinking. Some men does drink every day, from morning till night. Some men does drink every evening, from the time they finish work at five o'clock until whatever hour they decide to go home. Some men does drink only on weekends. But all men does drink more than the average Canadian or Amurcan. There is something about the weather, the humidity, rum-drinkers tell me, that does help with their enormous capacity for rum.

"All this sweating, man," they say, "all this humidity! The rum pours out o' your body through your pores. Free as sweat. We sweats-out the rum we imbibes!"

Frozen in Time ...

This summer I had the pleasure of spending two months with my mother at her suburban home in Mount Laurel, New Jersey, a place of huge lawns of green grass cut and watered expertly by serious Amurcan technology. I spent these two months drinking enormous quantities of "soda" and "spritzer" in the company of three of my five brothers (the other two live in Brooklyn); playing dominoes all day and all night while our mother warned us about the noise we made as we played ("Don't slamm the damn dominoes so hard, man!"); and cooking enormous amounts of food; "family packs" of steaks and pork chops and chicken parts and turkey wings. My three brothers — one a graduate of John Jay Law College, working now as a carpenter, another a medical student, the third an airline pilot — and I cooked enough food to feed an army, an expression my mother herself used to use when I was, for the first nineteen years of my life, the only child in the house. Back then, it was a smaller house, with no barbecue pit, no swimming pool, no two-car garage, no "motto-car." But the kitchen was almost half the side of our house, and her instructions about cooking were sharp and stentorian. She assumed that parental, superior attitude that left no possibility of independence of variation, of personal assurance, because my assurance was hers, my self-assurance came from her dignity of meaning, and from her memory of that history and her understanding of the myths that surround our ways of cooking.

Here I am now, in her house, in her kitchen — a fact to be taken into serious account — while her voice, still strong and piercing, assaults my ear. I am cooking African Chicken, a meal she has never herself cooked, a meal she has never tasted, a meal she will be having for the first time, and here she is telling me how much peanut butter to use, how many chicken parts to use, how much "seasning" to rub into the chicken parts.

"You sure you using the right ingreasements?"

I pretend I do not hear her. Her voice still bores disquiet and some small resentment into the body of the grown-up child, for the mother does not acknowledge, and is perhaps incapable of acknowledging, her child's maturity.

"Boy, I don't have to know exactly the thing you cooking." It is a kind of concession. "I don't have to know the ins and outs. Cooking is cooking! Why you don't rub some more lime-juice on the chicken? To take-way the freshness? Why you don't pour-on a lil more salt? Who you cooking for, though? For people that suffering from the pressure? Boy, season the chicken good, do!"

And I remember just in time, before I disrespect her rigid marking out of the boundary of mother and child, that she is my mother, and that perhaps she does not really have to know about Africa or Africanization or black Amurcan nationalism or soul food to know that a chicken needs the proper "seasning" to make the ingreasements palatable and sweet when they are cooked. And I listen. I have to listen.

My three brothers are in the kitchen with us. And they are sniggering, but only under their breath, still out of respect for her. She cannot strike them into submission now. She had a severe stroke three or four years ago. It left her right side out of natural function. She drags her right foot, only slightly, and holds her right arm to her side, to her breast, as if she is holding me, a child, in my infancy, with love and with some pain (I assume this by her posture of dragging and limping, although she suffers no pain).

Other than "this small inconvenience, boy, this blasted stroke that I had a year ago," my mother shows no effects of age and is still strong and sturdy. Her manner and her voice and her eyes tell me and my brothers that she wishes she *could* still strike us into submission. She stands beside me as she used to stand so many years ago, in the backyard kitchen, and she repeats, almost word for word, the directions she used to order me about with fifty years ago. And I go back in my mind, through the sharpness of her voice, to the time when we were still in that small island, when everything around us was smaller and more natural, and grown on trees in our backyard.